W9-CFL-608

THE COMMUNITY TABLE

THE COMMUNITY TABLE

Effective Fundraising through Events

SUSAN COLE URANO

Swallow Press

Ohio University Press

ATHENS

WITHDRAWN

FROM THE RODMAN PUBLIC LIBRARY

RODMAN PUBLIC LIBRARY

38212007166702
Rodman Main Adult
361.706 U72
Urano, Susan Cole, author
The community table

Swallow Press
An imprint of Ohio University Press, Athens, Ohio 45701
ohioswallow.com

© 2018 by Ohio University Press
All rights reserved

To obtain permission to quote, reprint, or otherwise reproduce
or distribute material from Swallow Press / Ohio University
Press publications, please contact our rights and permissions
department at (740) 593-1154 or (740) 593-4536 (fax).

Printed in the United States of America
Swallow Press / Ohio University Press books
are printed on acid-free paper ⊗™

28 27 26 25 24 23 22 21 20 19 18   5 4 3 2 1

Page ii: A team of volunteers served guests
at Bounty on the Bricks in Athens, Ohio.
Page x: Bounty on the Bricks featured entertainment
by a number of musicians, including this accordion player.
Both photographs courtesy of Dan Kubus

Paperback ISBN: 978-0-8040-1180-8
Electronic ISBN: 978-0-8040-4076-1

Library of Congress Control Number: 2018954509

This book was made possible in part through generous funding from the Athens County Foundation.

Dedicated to all the people I know who do the work of strengthening our communities and nonprofits

CONTENTS

PREFACE

THIS BOOK is a guide to planning a successful fundraising event in your community. Some of the ideas come from an event, Bounty on the Bricks, held in my community and originally sponsored by the Athens County Foundation. I also share suggestions from my experience planning other events and from fundraisers I've attended. I hope that you will find something of use in these pages that will help to raise money for organizations and causes you care about.

When my friend Cheryl suggested putting on a locally sourced meal for four hundred guests on the main street of our town, I knew immediately that it would work! The fundraising event that developed from her idea would provide money to benefit hungry people in our community. One board member reacted to the idea by saying, "I knew this was a project that fit the foundation's mission." The energy, vision, and skills that Cheryl and her team brought to planning the event had the additional benefit of dramatically raising the visibility of the Athens County Foundation in the community while raising funds to support the local food pantries and the regional foodbank.

The Athens County Foundation (ACF) is a nonprofit that serves people and organizations in Athens County. It was founded in 1980 by Claire O. Ping, the first lady of Ohio University, as a way to preserve wealth within the community and support its citizens. The foundation's assets generate income for grants and community-leadership work. ACF provides a vehicle for the county's citizens to invest in their community while maintaining a connection to where their money is deployed. It brings people "to the table" to help solve some of our area's toughest problems.

Money is only one of the foundation's resources. Our community leadership activities provide a way for citizens to become involved in important issues such as those concerning health, town-gown collaboration, the area farmer's market, and facilities planning for public education. This fundraiser aligned perfectly with our initiative: to feed hungry people.

One of the best things about working for a community foundation is you never know what gift will walk through the door. The day Wendy and Cheryl came bounding in to tell me about a picture they had seen on Facebook was my lucky day! The town in the online post was Jonesborough, Tennessee. In the photograph hundreds of people are seated for a meal at one long table on a brick-paved downtown street. It is dusk; the table is aglow. "Why," Cheryl asked, "can't we do this here?"

Within a week, she agreed to chair an event that would be hosted on our historic brick-paved Court Street in Athens, Ohio. The Athens County Foundation board quickly decided to proceed with planning for Bounty on the Bricks; two other foundation partners were invited to join the effort. Our goal was to raise money to be used to help food pantries in our region serve healthy (fresh and frozen) food. With our purpose closely aligned with the work of the foundation and two funding partners on board, we were ready to begin.

That first year, Bounty on the Bricks raised $75,000 to invest in the SEO Foodbank and Kitchen, a division of Hocking Athens Perry Community Action (HAPCAP). An estimated two tons of food were delivered to approximately forty-two thousand people in seven counties.

Over one hundred volunteers worked hard to make the fundraiser successful. But a core team did most of the work. I am filled with awe and gratitude for each contribution toward the success of the event. But I particularly want to thank Cheryl Sylvester for her gracious, tenacious, and enthusiastic leadership, as well as Wendy Jakmas, Liz Turman, Cindy Hayes, Kim Jacobs, Shawna Stump, Mike Carpenter, Jane Means, Juli Miller, John Gutekanst, Alfonso Constriciani, Matt Rapposelli, Francis McFadden, Chelsea Hindenach, Hillarie Burhans, Paula Mosely, Katie Schmitzer, Asti Payne, Tyler Bonner, Jennifer Yanity, Shannon Pratt-Harrington, Polly Creach, Eva Bloom, Michelle Oestrike, Ron Lucas, Rich Campetelli, Sonya Ivancic, and the board and staff of the Athens County Foundation for their hard work and vision.

The idea for this book came from my friend and publisher Gillian Berchowitz. I appreciate her gentle nudge to write it. I would never have finished without the patient coaching and feedback of Ricky Huard, acquisitions editor of Swallow Press. I have been fortunate to have worked with some amazing mentors and attribute most everything I know about fundraising to them: Martie MacDonell, Sally and Walter Rugaber, Claire Ping, and Carol Kuhre. And I'm forever grateful for my patient and supportive husband, David.

INTRODUCTION

START WITH a purpose. All fundraising events are based on a great idea, but the decision to undertake the huge amount of work needed to succeed depends on why you do it. Is the cause something you care about? Does the fundraiser align with the mission and work of the organization? Does it have a compelling purpose? Events can be an important component of any nonprofit organization's fundraising plan, especially if you are looking to build visibility and community. But they are also a lot of work and have the lowest return on investment of any fundraising strategy. This book details how to put on a successful event by highlighting your community's assets and, on a deeper level, by considering how events can build and strengthen community, especially in small and midsize rural towns.

Bounty on the Bricks was held to raise dollars to feed people. In our region of Appalachia, some people do not have the ability to feed their family on a regular basis and are increasingly dependent on food pantries. Many residents don't have access to fresh food or possess the skills to prepare a meal from scratch.

Athens County is the poorest county in the state of Ohio. Located in the northern part of the Central Appalachian region of the United States, the county faces many of the same challenges as counties in West Virginia, eastern Kentucky, Tennessee, western Virginia, and North Carolina. The region is still struggling with the costs of historic extraction industries: poor air and water quality, environmental decay, and long-term unemployment. Athens County is a hotbed of opioid and heroin addiction and suffers from their effects on families, babies, the workforce, and health and from the resulting increase in crime.

Athens, a county of about sixty-six thousand people, is the most economically divided county in the state. About 20 percent of our residents and 30 percent of our children live at or below the poverty level. Almost one-third of the population is classified as food insecure; 61 percent do not have handy access to a grocery store.

People are hungry throughout Athens County. In 2013, Feeding America reported approximately 21 percent of Athens County residents were struggling to obtain enough food to feed their family—compared to 15 percent in Ohio and 17 percent in the nation. That means almost 13,820 of our neighbors struggle to put meals on the table each day. The Ohio Association of Foodbanks estimates that food-pantry visits increased in the county by 66 percent between 2006 and 2014. Over half of Athens County children are currently eligible for free or reduced-price lunch, compared to 45 percent in Ohio, according to the National Center for Education. Because children move through the school system, their hunger is more visible than that of adults. More programs exist to feed children during the school year, but during breaks and over the summer, they lose access to this food.

The first year of the fundraiser, a donor sponsored a screening of *A Place at the Table,* a film about hunger in the United States narrated by the actor Jeff Bridges. The public was invited to see the film the evening prior to the event. Ohio Foodbanks director Lisa Hamler Fugate spoke afterward and facilitated an audience discussion on feeding the hungry in Ohio.

Event volunteer coordinator Liz shared, "I always like to do stuff for the community. I think seeing the movie the first year, *A Place at the Table,* really changed my perception about hunger and poverty. I have teacher friends who tell me about the kids that go hungry in their classrooms. I think it's cool that everyone (on the committee) is so willing to help."

The food thread wove our mission of building a healthy, inclusive community into the idea of presenting a community meal, thereby raising funds for our region's foodbank. We knew that the foodbank, which supplies over seventeen food pantries in seven counties, was a stable, effective, well-run organization. This gave us the confidence we needed to recommend that proceeds go to support its work. We listened to the staff's expertise, and the foodbank became a strong partner. We worked closely with the staffs of our other partner foundations to identify and track their funding and to measure its effect on the community.

Fundraisers and nonprofit leaders are always on the prowl for new ideas, new ways to engage donors and community. But this work is important to the health of a community in ways that go beyond the money generated. This book provides specific information on how to put on a successful fundraising event by highlighting community assets and, on a deeper level, considers how this work builds and strengthens the community.

People who work at nonprofits, serve on nonprofit or religious boards, work as professional fundraisers and development staff, lead community change, belong to a community group, or work in philanthropy will benefit from this book. They will learn what is needed to mount a successful event, including when and why to put on a fundraiser, and when not to. Each chapter treats in detail and chronological order a key component in the process. Worksheets are included to help plan an event.

Teamwork is the engine that drives the work of fundraising events. Chapter 1 begins with that engine: How should you choose your people? It describes whom you need to build a strong team of capable community leaders and where to find them. It shares the characteristics of a good team and shows how to build trust and confidence. Good teams develop over time. They solve problems and manage conflict in creative ways that respect all their voices. Their volunteers have fun and celebrate success together!

Chapter 2 looks at the valuable role of volunteers in fund-raising success. How do you ask people to give of their time when they are busy? Who is likely to say yes? How will they work together? It outlines how to plan an effective meeting, resolve conflicts, and create an atmosphere of community.

Where do great ideas come from? That is explored in Chapter 3. Where *do* you find good fundraising ideas? What unique attributes of your community can be used to mount a successful event? How are ideas tested? What approach has the potential to generate both money and goodwill? What ones are inspirational?

Once you have decided on what event to hold, the next step is to draft a realistic and comprehensive budget. How much is needed? What will people pay? What else can boost profits? Chapter 4 deals with income and expenses. What are the possible sources of income? What expenses will you need to consider? What is the value of the event? Who authorizes expenses; who writes the checks? How does money travel through the organization? Who is really accountable?

Chapter 5 focuses on marketing. It explores what media people look at and respond to, and explains the importance of crafting a compelling message. What graphics align with the purpose of your event? Will video enhance your message? How will your community know what happened and who made it happen?

How do you enhance your potential revenue? What other options to capture profit exist? Who will pay for it all? These questions are answered in chapters 6 and 7. Chapter 6 covers the basics of sponsorships and their key role in financial success. Who are likely sponsors and why do we need them? How are they approached and for what amount? What do they get in return? Why shouldn't they be given everything they ask for? How do you recognize sponsors and thank them for their help in your success? How should you collect their contributions? What is the value of a sponsorship? How should you treat competitive businesses? Can your and your sponsor's promises be kept?

Most community problems are too big for one organization to solve alone. Often several are working to deal with the same issues. This concept of collaboration can apply to fundraising events. Chapter 7 explores potential partnerships that may enhance and even amplify your success. You'll learn how to construct a successful collaboration—from letters of agreement to joint celebration.

The next step is staging the event. In Chapter 8, event logistics are treated in detail, including timelines, regulations, location, food, supplies, rentals, permits, sound, and accessibility —the million details that require your attention. Where will guests park? What is your liability? The list can seem endless, but the worksheet contained within the chapter should help a logistics chair sort through the items in order of importance and sequence.

Guests almost always need food and refreshment. Whether you are providing water coolers and granola bars at a 10K race, or serving a seven-course meal with champagne at a formal gala, the best way to welcome and show hospitality to guests is to feed them. Chapter 9 covers food and beverages. What rules and regulations will you have to deal with? What will be served and how? Are warming, cooling, and cooking facilities needed? And, in today's world, how are special diets taken into consideration?

Chapter 10 explores different ways performers and entertainment can add value to your fundraising event. How do you begin to scout possible entertainers? How much should you pay? Do they require special care? If yes, who is in charge of that? What kind of special equipment might be needed?

Chapter 11 presents ways to tell your story. How do you construct a compelling message? When is the right time to share it? We've all been to events where the speakers drone on while our stomachs growl and our eyelids start to droop. What is a realistic attention span for guests? This chapter shows different ways to get your message across at the actual fundraiser.

Chapter 12 offers ways you can increase your profit during an event. It gives specific details about on-site auctions, raffles, the sale of related merchandise, and approaches for soliciting additional donations from your guests.

Chapter 13 explores how to share results and lessons learned and celebrate success. I provide insights and illustrations from past fundraisers and detail the building blocks to mount your own event so as to maximize your values, goals, and intention. I share stories from my thirty years of experience of the ups and downs of community fundraising and include interviews of key committee people, sponsors, foundation partners, and guests.

There is another, often unanticipated outcome of community event fundraising. Sharing a meal with neighbors knits us together in a dense web of support for those in need and enhances our identity as a community. Community fundraising builds relationships; those relationships determine our vitality as a town. An intricately connected community can weather most storms.

What's good for building community is good for philanthropy. In *Bowling Alone: The Collapse and Revival of American Community*, Robert Putnam observes, "volunteering is among the strongest predictors of philanthropy, and vice versa."[1] "In round numbers, joiners are nearly ten times more generous with their time and money than non-joiners. Social capital is a more powerful predictor of philanthropy than is financial capital."[2] Peter Block, in *Community: The Structure of Belonging*, states, "The context that restores community is one of possibility, generosity, and gifts, rather than one of problem solving, fear, and retribution."[3] Feeling connected allows a new conversation to take place—one focused on possibilities rather than problems. It requires citizens to act authentically and to choose to exercise power as a collective

---

1. Robert D. Putnam, *Bowling Alone: The Collapse and Revival of American Community* (New York: Simon & Schuster, 2000), 118.

2. Ibid., 120.

3. Peter Block, *Community: The Structure of Belonging* (Oakland, CA: Berrett-Koehner, 2009), 29.

rather than relinquish voice to a select few. This cultivates a space where all voices can be heard and collective decisions made that are in the best interest of the community.

A great fundraiser builds on our community's assets to lift those who need a little help in this world. In the process we continue to reinforce our dense web of social connection. We celebrate each other's successes, share our talents, and have fun together. But that's not all. Lew Felstein, retired director of the New Hampshire Charitable Foundation, said, "We must learn to view the world through a social capital lens. We need to look at front porches as crime-fighting tools, treat picnics as public health efforts, and see choral groups as occasions of democracy. We will become a better place when assessing the impact of social capital becomes a standard part of decision making."

Fundraising events can be a recipe to build social capital in a community. They offer citizens a reason to work together, to celebrate their assets, and to shine. The results can be improved food access, stronger relationships, and denser networks and webs of communication. And the "profit" goes way deeper than the money raised. The true profit is a healthier, more positive community that can take pride in its accomplishments. This profit takes our attention away from mere problem solving and leads it toward a celebration of who and where we are as a people.

EVENTS CAN be an important part of a fundraising plan. But there are good reasons not to do a fundraiser as well. Events don't usually raise a lot of money compared to individual donations, and they don't necessarily build loyalty to your organization. One obstacle to your success can be the lack of access to good volunteers! Most events work best with a full team of committed, excited volunteers who will plan the event, raise the sponsorships, sell the tickets, and do the work it takes to "set the table" for your guests. If volunteers are not available, don't plan a fundraiser.

Don't hold a fundraiser if your organization is in financial crisis. Successful fundraising events take a long time to plan, usually a year. They enlist a tremendous amount of volunteer and staff time. And they don't raise the kind of money an organization can generate by directly asking donors and receiving a check. Besides, it's hard to have fun when in crisis.

The main reason to do a fundraiser is to have fun, raise your visibility, and attract new supporters to your mission. If the board is worried about how the organization will continue to survive, if they have to lay off staff or go out of business, a fundraiser is not the answer.

If you are not in crisis and have a strong core of volunteers and a creative, fun idea, then you're ready. Now, let's look at how your idea to raise money aligns with your purpose for the greatest impact!

CHAPTER ONE

Ask the Right People

TEAMWORK

My best piece of advice is to find the right chair! When the Roanoke Valley Arts Council undertook a fundraiser in conjunction with the opening of the new regional airport, we knew that a well-connected committee was the only way we could raise the big sum of money budgeted for a new arts fund. We worked for several weeks carefully selecting each member of the committee, considering the talent and resources each could bring to the table. The woman we approached to chair the event was married to the contractor who built the airport. We knew she was a high-powered and well-organized leader with great connections in the community. The committee decided on a travel theme and got to work planning the gala. We didn't know our new chairwoman loved Cajun music. When she paid to bring one of the leading Cajun bands in the country to play at the opening, the result was an event that will be etched in the memories of the guests for years to come!

The Bounty on the Bricks committee sets up the day of the event.
Photo courtesy of Jo Carpenter

The predictor of a fundraiser's success is the quality of the team assembled to do the work. An effective chair is the glue that holds the team together and steers its members to success. A chair should be well connected in the community and have those phone numbers that allow access to the resources needed to pull the community together to do the work. A good chair understands the mission of the organization and how the money raised will be used to improve the community. This person can articulately and passionately tell your story. A good chair will be highly praised and sought after, yet motivated, not by praise, but by the community's needs. This individual has the skills to organize and motivate people to get the job done—not by micromanaging—by empowering others to rise to the occasion.

Finding the right person to chair a fundraising event sets the stage for success. Look for someone who has demonstrated leadership or potential leadership ability—the capacity to understand and motivate people, see the big picture, and hold a clear vision of success. A strong leader is a master delegator who makes every

Bounty on the Bricks event chair, Cheryl Sylvester, and her husband Tony arrive the night of the event.

Photo courtesy of Jo Carpenter

member feel as though each contribution is invaluable to the success of the event. A good leader knows when to roll up the sleeves and pitch in and when to stand back and let others work through challenges. This person is not afraid of conflict.

Our Bounty on the Bricks chair honed her leadership skills over years of running a large insurance office while managing her family businesses at the same time. She is as comfortable at a black-tie gala as at a corn-hole-pitching barbeque in the backyard. She finds everyone she meets intriguing and is a great listener, asking clarifying questions and making connections. She probably wouldn't write a $50,000 check for a name band, but she's a woman of integrity that no one can say no to!

The event chair is a volunteer, possibly a member of the organization's board. Although people working in business and the corporate world are usually considered desirable, don't overlook other folks who support your cause, have strong leadership ability, and are well liked in the community. Remember, the added value of fundraising events is to connect and build community. Those connections last far beyond the dollars raised.

Who should ask someone to chair an event? Ideally, the invitation should be delivered by a representative of the nonprofit, either the CEO or the board president. When you approach prospective chairs, emphasize the potential benefits of the fundraiser on the mission of the organization or the community. Because these people are accustomed to seeing the "big picture," they will understand the need that exists in your community and the potential value of the additional money that a fundraiser could generate. They enjoy fundraising and inviting others to become involved in an event. When you ask, be direct and clear about the responsibilities of the position.

The first job of the event chair is to decide what subcommittees are needed, what their job descriptions are, and who would be best to chair each. Subcommittees, a great way to disperse the many tasks of a fundraiser so that all the work doesn't fall on the

THE FUNDRAISING chairperson is responsible for coordinating and planning an event to raise money for your organization or cause. The chair will recruit and develop volunteers to help with the planning, setup, and teardown of the event. The workload for this position will be intense throughout the entire year. To be successful, the chair must develop and use systems that allow volunteers to participate with minimal direction when helping with fundraising events.

Tasks

1. Develop strategy to implement fundraiser.
2. Invite volunteers to fill committee positions.
3. Work with CEO or board chair to secure sponsorships for the event from local businesses.
4. Work with auction chair (if applicable) to secure donated items to sell.
5. Work with marketing chair and staff to ensure timely and accurate information about the event reaches the public.
6. Network in the community to generate support, enthusiasm, and attendance.
7. Oversee work of subcommittees.
8. Implement event in a timely and successful manner.
9. Celebrate success.
10. Evaluate event results and prepare recommendations for next year.

Qualities and Abilities of a Fundraising Event Chair

1. Motivates: Keeps the focus of the group on the outcome of the event.
2. Plans Strategically: Can see what needs to happen and asks the right people to carry it out.
3. Uses Diplomacy: Fluidly interacts with different people in the community.
4. Communicates: Is clear, easy to understand, and transparent in all interactions.
5. Delegates: Empowers and motivates others to do the work.
6. Oversees: Works within a budget and in a timely manner.
7. Fundraises: Is not afraid to ask for money!

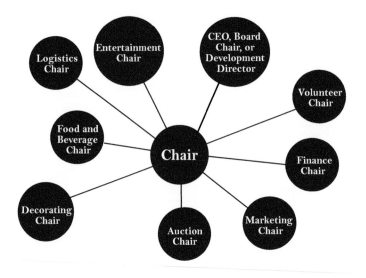

chair, could include the following: volunteer coordination, finance, food and beverage, decoration, logistics, marketing and ticket sales, and entertainment. If you are having an auction as part of your event, you'll also need an auction chair. The chair and sub-chairs will serve as the group that plans and makes most of the decisions about the fundraiser. However, some decisions will have an impact on the sponsoring nonprofit and will need to be made jointly with the CEO or board chair. For instance, licensing will need to be done through the nonprofit. Most major financial decisions are also the responsibility of the nonprofit. (*See sample organizational chart above.*)

Written job descriptions with enough detail about deadlines and lines of communication will be invaluable to the chair and subchairs. These could include their main tasks, the amount of time they have to accomplish the tasks, the available budget and income goal, who they will work with, what they will need to do the work, and how success will be measured.

Next, each subchair can begin recruiting a team of volunteers. The following paragraphs treat the general responsibilities of each committee and give some ideas about what skills are needed to fill each role.

The volunteer coordinator seeks people to do all the tasks necessary for the fundraiser: selling tickets, setting up the event, hauling trash, serving guests, displaying auction items, tending bar, cleaning up, and returning the many borrowed items used at the event. A good coordinator is highly organized and calm, confident, and comfortable in almost any situation. He or she likes people, knows how to navigate egos and conflict, and has a good understanding of others' strengths and an ability to match those to the tasks at hand. This individual should be an excellent communicator, with the ability to give clear and precise instructions concerning tasks, dates, times, and locations. A coordinator may train volunteers or assign specific jobs to the subcommittee chairs, such as teaching how to set a proper place setting, how to time a race, or what constitutes an appropriate drink-serving size. People who have these skills are often teachers, coaches, nurses, and other members of "helping and teaching" professions. Above all, a good volunteer coordinator can thank, praise, and encourage easily, making everyone feel appreciated and that the success of the event was due in part to each volunteer's contribution!

The finance chair or treasurer will oversee expenditures and income. People who enjoy working independently with numbers and Excel spreadsheets are a good fit in this role. When looking for a finance chair, consider individuals who run their own businesses or work in banking or finance. The finance chair will often work in conjunction with a paid staff from, or the chief financial officer or executive director of, the sponsoring organization to design a budget and monitor expenses and income. Unless the fundraiser is independent of a nonprofit, the ultimate accountability falls on that nonprofit sponsor, and its representative may have to authorize expenditures, sign checks, and write thank-you letters to donors and sponsors. (An example of an independent fundraiser would be a club raising money for the Red Cross: the event would not be sponsored by the Red Cross, and the club isn't a legally incorporated entity.)

Marketing chairs should understand how people hear about events in their community. They develop promotional pieces and decide when and through what outlet these messages will be delivered. The marketing chair will be responsible for ticket sales or registrations, although this task can be assigned to a subcommittee of marketing. Choose someone with good communication skills, the ability to write a clear compelling message, and connections to media. Add an understanding of video, and you've got a dynamite chair! Sometimes this person can be found at a local newspaper or television or radio station. If you know someone who understands marketing, social media, and/or sales, ask him or her to chair this committee.

To find a volunteer to seek sponsors for the event, look for people who like to raise money in the community. These folks may have chaired or worked on local campaigns before. They are confident and not afraid to ask for money or goods—in fact, they enjoy talking to people. Sometimes the event chair, CEO, or development director will take on this responsibility. But I have seen highly effective committees raise sponsorships on their own quite effectively.

The logistics chair has a huge and invaluable job: to design where everything goes, including tables, bars, check-in stations, food service areas, tents, service lines, and trash cans. This chair works closely with the volunteer coordinator to find enough people to get the job done, checks in with the finance chair when ordering supplies for the event to align with the budget, and works with city and county officials or property owners to make sure everything complies with fire and health department regulations and provides access to adequate power and water sources. The logistics chair arranges for access to bathroom facilities, finds a place to store ice, and assigns parking for supply trucks. You need someone who is practical and detail oriented, yet able to visualize the big picture. This individual must be able to tackle problems head-on and negotiate solutions. Look for someone who already manages people or situations well, perhaps one holding a leadership role in an organization or running a private business.

The food and beverage coordinator works with the chefs, the caterers, or a restaurant to design a pleasing menu. If your event is a fancy meal, look for someone who *knows* food, possibly a person already in the industry or someone who likes to plan dinner parties. If food doesn't play a big role in your event, then this assignment is a simple volunteer job. Working with the food industry requires an ability to express clearly what is needed, negotiate prices, plan menus and determine what quantities of each item are needed, arrange for deliveries, and oversee serving requirements. Look for a creative person who understands the business of food!

Designing the look of the event is left to the decorating committee, often people who prefer hands-on jobs. Look for these folks in more creative parts of your community. Florists, party planners, or natural hosts are good choices. They will know what looks good and how to make your guests comfortable. I have found that one of the challenges of working with the decorating committee (and, sometimes, the food coordinator) is keeping costs within budgets. At one event I dealt with costs by using a local landscaper as a volunteer to create a gardenlike entryway in exchange for recognition. A tasteful card strategically located in the display pointed guests to the company and its contributions.

Good entertainment volunteers know the industry and are comfortable inviting performers, negotiating fees and contracts, and determining staging requirements. Look for performers, presenters, or other artistic folk to chair this committee.

Once the subchairs are in place, they can begin to form their own teams. Some volunteers will come through the nonprofit and be assigned a subcommittee; others will be recruited by the subchairs. The chair will call the subcommittee chairs together to

The event entryway was donated by Greenleaf Gardens Center.
Photo courtesy of Ben Siegel

schedule and coordinate most aspects of the event. How often the committee meets as a whole is up to the temperament of the group, but I suggest meeting no more than once or twice a month. Most of the work should be done on the subcommittee level with only major decisions coming to the group of subchairs. It's important to respect a volunteer's time, so don't meet too often! Keep your meetings concise with brief reports, either written or oral, and allow time for addressing problems. Committee time should be spent addressing joint concerns, bringing up new ideas and solving problems. Don't micromanage! Keep brief minutes and share these with the committee before each meeting. Use them as a checklist for the following meeting to determine what needs to happen next.

Here's a glimpse of effective teamwork. During interviews about their experiences serving as a committee member of a recent fundraiser, everyone mentioned the ease with which the committee functioned. One volunteer said, "This is a good event, good cause. The chair is great at navigating. Everyone is here for the right reason. The event is highly organized. Everyone knows what their job is." Another member said, "The committee is really supportive. They agreed to the goals and are receptive to new ideas. They talk ideas through, are thoughtful. They integrate new ideas, are cooperative yet autonomous." How do you generate that level of cooperation?

A sense of community grows from the respect, trust, and friendships that develop within the group. The committee checks their egos at the door as they enter into the work of raising money to support their cause. There is no place at the table for self-aggrandizement and no spare energy to assuage the ego or promote the righteousness of a volunteer or guest. We've all worked on projects that derail because of the needs of one person, so pick your team carefully!

This takes time. A good event starts about one year out. This head start allows for time to assemble the perfect team, test ideas, and secure a date and venue. Every member has a chance to get to know the team, to explore their ideas with others, and to really listen. Questions and ideas are raised and worked through as a group. The time it takes to build cohesion and trust is not wasted time. Once in place, the group will navigate choppier waters with ease. And don't forget to throw in a little humor and make it fun!

Next look outside your committee for support. Call in a team! Thanks to the local football team who volunteered to tear down a local event, the street was cleared of fifty tables and four hundred chairs in about one hour after the event closed. Team members provided the muscle to hoist tables and huge stacks of chairs onto the truck returning them to the community center. They had fun, too! You will know what groups in your community you can count on to pitch in.

We often use volunteers to serve guests. These can include student groups from area high schools such as Key Club and

Volunteer servers often have as much fun as the guests!
Photo courtesy of Dan Kubus

cheer squads, church groups, and even board members of the nonprofit! Jennie has volunteered to coordinate servers for many events. She has worked in food and beverage service her entire life and knows what is needed to serve guests. Her job for us was to train seventy novice servers in one hour, many of them under eighteen years of age. She coached, joked, commanded, and managed to get five courses on the table for four hundred people in a timely manner. The young volunteers had fun being downtown and helping. Some mature volunteers prefer serving to sitting at the table! All are fed pizza, thanks to a local donation, and receive a great thank-you letter at the end.

When asked what advice she would have for another community wishing to mount a large event, one volunteer said, "Start early. Make sure everybody's on the same page. Organize. Document everything well. Assign specific roles for volunteers."

Don't be afraid to ask volunteers to join your committee. Most will say that when it's all over they received more than they gave. One person said, "When I first joined the committee as

COMMITTEE	TRAITS OF CHAIR	DUTIES	LENGTH OF COMMITMENT	NUMBER OF RECRUITS NEEDED
Chair	Connected, respected person with strong leadership skills	Assembles committee, chairs meeting, meets with sub chairs, fundraises, liaisons with organization CEO, serves as spokesperson for the event	From beginning to end	Full committee
Volunteer Chair	Personable, thorough, respectful, good communicator	Recruits, trains, supervises, and thanks volunteers for helping	From beginning of planning to after thank-you notes are sent	Usually none
Treasurer	Numbers person, knows Excel, understands profit and pricing, reliable, honest, accountable	Drafts and monitors budget, approves changes and assures profitability	From beginning of planning to final bill is paid	Usually none
Sponsorship	Outgoing, confident, good communicator, well connected, likes to fundraise	Following sponsorship plan, drafts a proposal for different giving levels, meets face to face with potential donors, secures gifts	From beginning until all sponsorships are in place, usually a few months	Could use a team
Logistics	Highly organized with an ability to keep the big picture in mind, understands sequencing and processes	Develops maps, blueprints, timelines, procurement and permits	From beginning through clean up and return of all items	Team of three to five
Entertainment	Someone who knows the industry or has booked acts before	Suggests, secures, and facilitates entertainment	Can start later in the process unless looking for a national act	None
Auction	Similar to sponsorship: connected to the community, not afraid to ask for donations	Secures auction items and plans auction for success	Starts early and works through the event	Team of five
Decoration	Creative individual who likes parties	Plans the look of the event	Starts early and works through the event	Team of five
Marketing	Possesses marketing skills: writing, design, messaging, media	Plans messages, determines outlets and sequencing of information and invitations	Starts early and works through the event	None
Food and Beverage	Someone in the industry with experience working with caterers or someone who likes to cook	Plans the food and beverages	Starts early and works through the event	Team or solo

JENNIE IS a master storyteller. She shared, "I've been head of service for the event. It's a very stressful job! It's not just the volunteers who are young and have no experience, but it's wrangling the chef and service to make a huge transition. I have to be tough enough to make sure everything gets done and nice enough that nobody's crying! It's the heat of the moment! My goal is to maintain balance."

logistics chair, I didn't know what was meant by logistics. I've grown through this process, learned as I went about how to do something like this together. We prepared for mistakes, so there was little panic. Different views, opinions, strengths, and weaknesses are at the table, and we were able to learn from one another because of our diversity. The work provides opportunities to have contact with different facets of our community. There are no large egos to contend with. It's a safe environment to share ideas."

SUMMARY

1. Start early, up to one year ahead, to put together your ideas and team leadership.
2. CEO or president finds the best chair available, someone who can see the big picture, inspire others, and ask!
3. Develop subcommittee job descriptions.
4. CEO and chair identify and recruit subchairs, carefully matching a volunteer's skills to a position.
5. Avoid micromanaging volunteers; reward their efforts and support their work.
6. Develop goals and a timeline for the event through its completion. Share both with all volunteers.

7. Build trust and safety within the committee by allowing each voice a place.

8. Take good, concise minutes and distribute those in a timely fashion.

9. Make meetings fun! Set a regular meeting schedule and keep meetings brief.

10. Deal with conflict directly and fairly.

CHAPTER TWO

The More the Merrier

VOLUNTEERS

MOST EVENTS require an army of enthusiastic volunteers. When I'm asked to help with something, I will usually say yes, especially if a friend calls. When Beth called her friend Meredith, a local high school cheerleading coach, to see if she could commit her team to volunteering a few hours of their time to serve dinner, Meredith readily agreed. She was happy her friend thought of her. She could see that this would fill a community service mission for her team and give the members a valuable experience to add to their resumes as they prepared for college applications. The night of the event, twelve girls reported for duty in white shirts and black skirts, worked hard without complaint, and had a great time. Some even earned tips for their good service.

The volunteer coordinator works with the committee to recruit people for each team. The first recruitment task, once the event chair is in place, is to find the subchairs. The table in chapter 1 gives some ideas about what people to ask for which jobs

Chef Alfonso Constriciani with his team of volunteer servers
Photo courtesy of Joe Bell

and where to find them. The committee chair, CEO, or board chair will, most likely, identify a few candidates and contact them to ask for their help. Keep in mind that contacting prospects by email or snail mail is too impersonal, creating the perception that you couldn't take the time to contact them in person. Most people prefer to be asked in person or on the phone. Online volunteer recruitment tools can work for some large projects or service clubs. If you're working with younger folks, this vehicle will appeal to them, but not to the over-fifty crowd. What these programs lack is the conversation that allows you to make the best match, adjust the terms of the commitment, and ensure the loyalty of the volunteer. For instance, I went online to volunteer for a local event. But the shifts were four hours long in the sun. I would have committed to two hours, but there was no way to let the organization know that. Even more important, I wouldn't have felt obligated to my shift, if I committed through an online portal. But if my friend called, I would be sure I followed through with my decision.

When you meet with the prospects, come with exact details about what you want them to do, complete with a job description, time requirement, and information as to whom they will be working with. Let a prospect know the dates and length of commitment and whom to report to. Once the subchairs are in place, they can begin to recruit their own people. These will most often be their friends or people they feel comfortable working with —but not always. I have intentionally invited strangers to work together on a committee. Working together on a time-limited project around shared values is a strong community-building exercise. If you know your people, then you know their comfort level with the unknown. Some subcommittees, such as finance, won't need extra help. Others, like decorating, will need many hands to get the job done!

Where do you find volunteers? Most people start with their friends. Your friends might enjoy working on a project with you, or they might align around a shared cause. Beyond friends, think of the groups you are involved with or have connections to. Do you belong to a church or a social or community service club? See if any other members might join you. If you need big groups of people, look for groups of young people. Members of sports teams, foreign language clubs, student council, cheerleading squads, and key clubs are all looking for community service projects. Be aware that the further out of your sphere of influence you look for volunteers, the more chance there is of them not showing up or following through. I have found this particularly true with college students. One way to plan for no-shows is to schedule more people than you think you'll need.

Understanding the many reasons why people volunteer may help you with recruiting. They may see themselves as "helping" people, or they may want credits for their resumes. Most people have fun working on a community project with others. They enjoy the camaraderie, make new friends, and feel good. Some people volunteer to set an example, for either their employees or their children. Others like knowing the inside scoop and learning first-hand about an event. The prestige associated with the event or in being seen in the community motivates a few folks. Retirees can be fabulous volunteers because they have both the time and the experience to be valuable contributors, and they often enjoy being with others. And some people volunteer because they believe deeply in your cause. All of these are valid reasons to volunteer; understanding your volunteer's motivation will help you place him or her in the best position to satisfy both your needs..

Every now and then a fundraiser recruits people whose personal needs overshadow the event. You'll know who they are: They have opinions about everything. They are the self-appointed experts. At times, they seem to suck the air out of the room. I have seen events almost derailed by these big personalities. They are usually not aware of their effect on the group, but they can cause a lot of hard feelings. When this happens, the chair may want to have a private conversation with the troublemakers and ask them to be more aware of the impact of what they say. If that approach doesn't work, they may be asked to leave the committee. You don't want all your good work being tainted by a few dysfunctional volunteers.

Another caution involves using underage volunteers in situations involving alcohol. Sometimes a volunteer supervisor can structure the experience for the kids so that they are not directly serving or cleaning up alcohol at an event. Remember, the host organization is liable for any unlawful or excessive consumption or the accidents that might occur as a result. You want your volunteers to *feel* safe and *be* safe throughout the event.

Once your team is in place, take stock of what, if any, training is required. Do they need to know how to deal cards, time a race, mix a martini? If so, identify who will do the training and when. Clearly communicate this with the volunteer team. Let them know when and where they need to show up, what their job will be, what to wear, where to park, what will be expected of them, and when they will be done. It's always nice to feed your volunteers too! We have had pizza donated to feed the crew before an event. Be clear whether volunteers can or can't partake of the food and beverages served to guests at the event.

Finally, thank your volunteers—a lot! Thank them at the event—publicly if there's an opportunity. Send them a thank-you letter after the event. I've found that kids really appreciate these letters and even use them in their college applications. If it's appropriate, have a wrap-up event for everyone who worked on the fundraiser, giving them a chance to celebrate their success, see their friends, and reinforce their good feeling about helping out. You can use this meeting as an opportunity to gather feedback from your volunteers either verbally, or with a written or electronic questionnaire. These evaluations can be used to improve next year's event.

SUMMARY

1. Identify what volunteers are needed to serve—choosing subchairs first, then your subcommittee teams.
2. Develop a job description for volunteers with enough detail for them to be able to make a decision when asked.
3. Ask.
4. Provide a schedule of work with a timeline, detailing specific expectations.
5. Clearly communicate to your volunteers what they will be doing; when and where; what they should wear; where they can park; and when their work will be over.
6. Feed them.
7. Train them.
8. Thank them.
9. Ask for their feedback.

CHAPTER THREE

Great Ideas

EVENT CONCEPTS

WITH THE right team in place, the fun begins. Volunteers were selected to help carry out a fundraising idea, but once the creativity of the team emerges, the idea will change and evolve into a profitable and fun event. Where do ideas come from?

My best ideas came from adapting successful fundraisers held in other communities! Bounty on the Bricks originated from a Facebook post. From there it was up to the committee to make someone else's fundraiser work in our community. We had to identify what things made our community special, then determine how they could be featured in our event. Local foods and its rich history are important to our community, so the presence of a great culinary school at Hocking College and the historic, locally made brick streets formed the lens through which we shaped the plan. But the idea came from an image! Other ideas have surfaced from talking with colleagues, hearing speakers at conferences, and adapting successful popular media themes or shows such as *Dancing with the Stars*. There are very few truly original fundraising ideas. The ALS Ice Bucket Challenge seemed new and novel, and it was in its use of social media. But it was really a new take on an old idea of showing solidarity toward a cause: similar approaches have included shaved heads in support of chemo patients; and No Shave November, with men growing beards to raise awareness, support, and money for cancer patients.

The best place to start looking for an idea is to find other successful fundraisers and decide which ones would resonate with your community. Most ideas in the nonprofit fundraising world are up for grabs and can be found online, in books, and through word of mouth. Most nonprofit leaders are willing to share their strategies, plans, and budgets with you, if you ask. Look at nonprofit websites, search fundraising ideas, ask colleagues, and look around to see what is working for others.

Most fundraising ideas fall into several basic categories detailed in this chapter. Some take a year to plan and execute; others are put together quickly. The resources of your team and makeup of your community will help decide what will work best for you. If you are located in wine country and have several people from the industry on your committee, a wine auction is a natural. Start with what you have.

Let's start with auctions—a great way to make money, especially if all the items are donated. Auctions can be themed around just about anything: wine, trips, art, goods, and food. Auctions can be live, silent, online, or a combination of types. Because there is a thrill to bidding in person, live auctions generate the most excitement. You see whom you're bidding against, and the friendly rivalry generated often raises the take. Silent auctions are done either in person at an event or online. The item is displayed and people write or submit their bid. They can see what the highest bid is and respond quickly. Chapters 6 and 12 provide more details about putting on a successful auction.

Raffles can be held on their own or as a complement to an auction. Tickets are sold for a chance to win an item—usually a

At one fundraiser a wine tasting for twelve was placed on auction.
Photo courtesy of Brian Blauser

bigger item such as a car or a pot of money—to attendees or to people in the community. One or several winners are drawn either at the event or later.

Meals can bring the community together to benefit a shared cause or just in celebration. Breaking bread together builds

Nancy Pierce, director of the Calliope Feminist Choir, was named the 2018 Woman of the Year by the Women's Fund of the Athens County Foundation. *Photo courtesy of Athens County Foundation*

community. The giving and sharing of food is one of the oldest forms of caring and generosity. However, as there is more cost associated with hosting a meal as a fundraiser and the profit margin is generally less, most events that involve a meal have additional ways to generate income. A fundraising meal can be a breakfast, luncheon, or dinner. A successful Groundhog Day breakfast in Zanesville, Ohio, generates significant revenue for their community foundation! A luncheon honoring the "Woman of the Year" brings like-minded people together to celebrate powerful women who make a difference in our community. A dinner can be built around many themes—from Derby parties to New Year's celebrations. There are numerous ways to enhance profitability, but the basic fundraising tenets hold true for meals: Use as much donated food, labor, and decorations as you can. Always offer the best.

If you're planning a meal, consider your intended guests and shape the event around their convenience and taste. If you are holding a breakfast, you'll have a limited time frame in which to keep people's attention, so lengthy programs or elaborate auctions won't work. During the breakfast, be efficient, have plenty of coffee, and keep to your promised schedule. As quality and efficiency are at a premium, be cautious about using volunteer servers and chefs. Breakfasts cost less than dinner so paying for service is less daunting. Speakers should keep their messages short and concise, limited to no more than fifteen minutes. Keep in mind that most successful fundraising breakfasts make their money ahead of time through sponsorships and table sales.

Luncheons can be a lovely way to raise money, but unless your event is held on a weekend, they share many of the same constraints as breakfast. During the week, most people work and have trouble leaving their jobs for more than one to one-and-a-half hours for lunch. Lunch can be served or a buffet; it should always be planned for your guests' comfort and efficiency. Have a compelling focus to your luncheon such as recognizing volunteers, sharing your success, or bringing to light a compelling cause. Sweet teas or red-hat luncheons where ladies wear red hats can be great fun.

Dinners are more expensive and ask more of your guests, so you'll need to do more to be successful. Details on how to plan a successful dinner event or gala are woven throughout the following chapters. The advantage to a dinner is that guests have more time to relax, enjoy the event, and spend money on your cause!

Athens County Foundation's Athens Professionals for Philanthropy hold a
5K–10K Father's Day Race to promote and fund a summer feeding program.
Photo courtesy of Athens County Foundation

Whether your dinner is a western-style barbeque or a black-tie
gala, the key is to design an event that will be in demand.

Races are a common type of fundraiser and come in all forms:
5K–10K, walking, bicycling, motorcycle poker runs, wheelchair,
beds on wheels, and river rafts. People like to compete against
themselves and others in their group or community to benefit a
good cause and have great fun. Races often appeal to younger
volunteers and donors. Be aware that weather can be an important factor in the success of a race. An equally popular and similar form of fundraising is a tournament. Golf, four-square,
badminton, croquet, dance-offs, bowling—almost any game can
be made into a tournament. I worked for an organization that
once hosted a national jigsaw-puzzle tournament that generated
big money because people from far and wide vied for the title.

If you decide to mount a race or hold a tournament, learn as
much about the sport or event requirements as you can. Look at

Race for a Reason participants designate where their donations will go.
Photo courtesy of Lander Zook

what others have done. Are there rules and standards that you will need to adhere to? Will you need a referee? Does the playing field need to be an exact size or require a clean surface? Will your participants need space to warm up to get ready to compete? What are the safety precautions you need to take? Many races have an emergency medical team in place to treat injuries. These types of fundraisers can also seek profits through registration fees and sponsorships. Sometimes products, such as T-shirts and water bottles, can be sold at the event. Prizes and "goody bags" are often given. Both can reflect local culture; prizes can also be traditional medals or ribbons. If you plan to give your competitors a "goody bag," find a sponsor or charge a higher fee. Have a sponsor buy or donate your prizes. Hold an award ceremony at the end of the race to recognize everyone's accomplishments.

Night of the Legends, a local talent show, was held to support Stuart's Opera House in Nelsonville, Ohio. *Photo courtesy of Angie Boyd McDonald*

For those who love to perform, a revue or talent show can be a successful, if not all-consuming fundraising event. A revue brings local performers together for a series of dances, songs, and comedy acts connected by a loose storyline. A show will offer a spotlight for those with talent to share with the community. Performers and professionals donate their time and skills, and tickets are sold to the event. For either a revue or a show you will need some talent to hold the audience's attention, as well as the ability to organize a production, a venue to hold it in, and an event that people will want to come and see. Good, professional sound quality helps a production, and live music adds a layer of excitement!

Performances as fundraisers require a good venue—a theater or auditorium where lighting, sound, and seating can be managed. The comfort and convenience of your audience members (donors) need to be taken into consideration. Are there plenty of comfortable seats; are some handicap-accessible? Will you serve refreshments? Does the venue offer restrooms? Have you planned an intermission? Is convenient parking available?

Performers, who are donating their time and talents, should also be treated well. They are usually making an enormous personal commitment. I've heard that *Dancing with the Stars* events put a huge burden on the participants who are asked to buy costumes and take lessons: costs often range into thousands of dollars. A friend shared that she had to scavenge second-hand stores because she could not afford the high rental costs of a costume.

To cover your costs, sponsors are often the key to success. They can be a lead sponsor; buy an ad in a program; or pay for a specific expense such as theater rental, local advertising, or even the director's salary!

Galas are the cream of the crop in the fundraising event world and can command a high price for tickets. A gala can feature celebrity performers, fabulous food, alcohol, and dancing. If most of the event is donated, then proceeds can be high. Often galas will offer the guests additional ways to give including auctions, raffles, and outright requests for contributions and pledges. Guests are treated to the best of everything. A gala is a chance to spotlight your organization and gain a high visibility with very wealthy individuals.

If you choose a gala as your fundraiser, pull out all the stops. Don't skimp on food, drink, or entertainment. You'll want to serve a meal that is desirable to your intended audience. Offer moderate-to-better wines and a selection of drinks prepared by professional bartenders. Don't forget the coat-check service and, if necessary, valet service for parking cars. If you have dancing, prepare a dance floor on a harder surface with enough room for many of your guests to participate. Galas can feature big-name performers; if they believe in your cause, they may donate their services.

Gaming can be a fundraising event. Poker, Bingo, and casino nights are the most common form of this type of fundraiser. Your venue will be set up to look like a casino with gaming tables

Key Event offers guests a choice of color-coded keys, each matching a host home. The guests are given maps directing them to those homes for dinners prepared by volunteer chefs.

Photo courtesy of Brian Blauser

and dealers. You can sell chips and use a cashier for checking in and out. If possible, hire professionals who know what they're doing, but don't give all your profits away to them in the form of fees. Some groups hold gaming nights with all volunteers. Bingo games and raffles can be handled successfully this way. Remember, all gaming is considered a form of gambling. There are laws that govern gambling, so be sure to know what is required in your state.

Any of these ideas and their countless combinations and varieties can be crafted into a fundraiser that will work well in your community. Use the resources you have and the passions and talents of your community and committee, and see what ideas bubble up. One word of caution: make sure that your fundraiser doesn't go against the mission of the organization for which you are raising money. For example, you might not want to host an alcohol-heavy gala as a fundraiser for MADD (Mothers Against Drunk Driving).

Test your idea with friends in the community. Talk it up and see how people react. If it falls flat, go back to the drawing board.

SUMMARY

1. Know your community and what they enjoy and will support.
2. Look at what other nonprofits have done to raise money.
3. Pay attention to what ideas generate excitement with your committee and community.
4. Emphasize something unique about your community.
5. Combine several fundraising ideas into one event.
6. Know your committee, cause, and capabilities.
7. Test your idea out on friends and donors.
8. Start early.
9. Get as much donated for the event as possible.

CHAPTER FOUR

Raising Money

FINANCIAL GOALS

THE NET profit you seek is one of the most important pieces of the puzzle when creating a successful fundraiser. I have seen many fundraisers that start with enthusiasm and a genuine desire to help, but without careful planning and clear goals, end with low or no profit. Knowing how much money you want to raise will be your roadmap for pricing and purchasing. Here's how to carefully and realistically craft a budget before the work begins.

Say you want to raise money to send your school band to Disney World to perform. Their costs are $10,000 to cover the bus fare, hotels, and meals for the band members. As this is an unexpected opportunity for the band that isn't included in the school budget, parents decide to raise the money. The easiest way is to divide the total needed by the twenty band members and ask each to pay a share of $500. But one-third of the band members' families can't afford the cost. So parents decide to help. Their goal could be $3,500, or it could be the entire $10,000. Some of the parents like to cook, so they plan to hold bake sales at the football games. There are five games, so they need to raise $2,000 per game. But at $1 a brownie, it'll take two thousand brownies per game to reach their goal. Then one parent suggests taking orders at school for baked goods by the dozen, with delivery service available for an added fee. Say they charge $10 a dozen, or $15 with delivery. Now they need to sell 667 orders, or thirty-three orders per band member—still too much to expect. However, they could place a line for additional donations on the order form. As the parents are donating the ingredient costs, all proceeds will go to their goal. If they add a few other ideas to the mix, they can easily reach their $10,000 goal in less time, with less work.

Some parts of a budget are easy to calculate, like how much a caterer will charge, because you enter into a contract that details the cost of the service. Try to determine all your costs and include them in the budget. Then you can start to look at your projected income. Start with the price of a ticket or entry. Each community has a threshold for ticket prices that can only be exceeded with caution, particularly small towns and rural communities. Think of the principle of supply and demand: If the fundraiser is truly unique and exciting, tickets will be in high demand. In that case, you might try raising your price, remembering that it should match the demand and a buyer's perception of its value. In my hometown the highest ticket price is $150 per person, but every community is different. How many people can you accommodate? Multiply that by the price for the total ticket revenue.

So let's get started. First, list all your known expenses. These could include food or catering; rentals such as tables, tents, service, and tablecloths; liquor and other permits; advertising, including printed invitations; liquor; decorations, prizes, and T-shirts; insurance; and entertainment, including musicians. This will take some research. Go online and track down the actual costs. Put agreements or contracts in place if you can. Don't forget the cost of services you might not think about at first such as a sound system; miscellaneous supplies like trash bags, tape, and corkscrews; a photographer; or extra insurance. You can begin to fill in your budget in the provided sample chart. Once all costs are in place, add the goal or what you hope to raise to be successful. Now you can play with costs, tickets, and donations to develop a realistic total fundraising goal.

MY FIRST fundraising event was at a small arts organization in rural Ohio. It was there that I met my first mentor, Martie. She was a commanding, complex woman with silver hair and a huge smile. Working with Martie, I learned how to prepare a sponsorship proposal and build strong partnerships. She challenged me to think as big as possible, to harness my creativity, and to see ideas through to success.

In Virginia, Sally and Walter showed me how to think big, while bringing a strong business sense to the vision. Martie could rally support with her generous charisma; Sally and Walter planned for success. The hardest lesson I learned from them was how to walk away from a project that couldn't generate the income needed to be successful.

We researched mounting a Spoleto-type arts festival in Roanoke, Virginia, for nearly a year. We traveled to Charleston, South Carolina, twice to see how it was done. We talked to local businesses and artists. We had great ideas and plans! With the beauty of the Roanoke Valley and its abundance of creative people, how could we not succeed? We targeted one major corporation for our lead sponsor. Walter, then publisher of the Roanoke *Times and World News*, spent a day talking to its CEO. We thought that the corporation's need for goodwill would make this event appealing, a "no brainer"! But at the end of the day, the CEO's response was that the fundraiser was not a good fit for his company's corporate mission. We made the hard decision to walk away from our plans. Without a firm commitment of underwriting from the lead sponsor to offset the cost, the project would have lost considerable money and not been sustainable in the long run.

Once you have your fixed costs, you can play around with income and ticket price. If the community will support a $75 ticket price per person and the capacity of the event is four hundred, then tickets will generate $30,000. If your goal is to raise $25,000 dollars, then all is well, right? Not quite. If the total meal cost is $25,000, you are left with a profit of $5,000. Fundraisers are a huge commitment of time, resources, and community goodwill. A $5,000 profit from four hundred people, each paying $75, is not an acceptable return on investment. If the goal of the event is to raise $30,000, then an additional $25,000 needs to be raised.

How much profit makes for success? A consultant once told me to never do an event for under $15,000 profit. That was thirty years ago. Today, consider $30,000 as a minimum goal, depending on the size of your community. Again, your profit must justify the time, effort, and social capital needed to mount a magnificent event.

There are many ways to close the gap between costs and profit in a budget. The ticket price could be raised, but carefully consider your market and your risk if the community won't spend what you ask for a ticket. Pricing your event is a tough decision. You'll hear many varied opinions. Just remember, you are planning a fundraising event, not a charity service. You will undoubtedly hear that there are people who can't afford to come or who should get free tickets. Go back to your original intent—to raise money for a worthy cause. The more successful you are at meeting your financial goal, the more your community will benefit. If the ticket cost is $80 instead of $75, that's $2,000 more raised from your four hundred guests.

Selling alcohol can boost profits as well. Determine what you want to sell and how much it will cost. Do you want to sell cans of beer or pour from a keg? How many types of wine will you offer? Can guests buy a bottle? One local fundraiser offers a "special designer" cocktail—something new each year—and charges a premium price to guests. Once you determine your costs and price for each guest, you can plug both into your budget. In our example, if $3,000 is netted from alcohol sales, then $20,000 remains to reach the $30,000 net profit goal! The next step is to look at sponsors.

Local businesses often enjoy the visibility a highly successful fundraiser offers them. Consider inviting sponsors to join you in your fundraising goal to assure your success. The "sell" is made easier if your event is for a worthy cause such as feeding the hungry. Be careful when selling sponsorships not to give away the store to your sponsors and, as a result, eat into your profits—especially by handing out free tickets. If you do offer perks to your sponsors, be sure to include them in your budget. For instance, if you offer a sponsor seating for a table of eight at your event, you will have eight fewer tickets to sell, or $640 less income.

Look for an anchor sponsor, one with the ability to contribute the largest amount in return for the greatest visibility. In our example, $5,000 secures the anchor position. For this donation, the sponsor gets top billing on all promotions around the event. The perks may include a seat of honor, a table at the front of the room, or other recognition of the sponsor's support at your event. In a large city, the cost of a lead sponsorship might be much higher. Following this example, the next-level goal could be two sponsors at $2,500 each. They receive second billing and smaller perks. A third tier of sponsors, contributing between $500 and $1,000, can be invited to help you make up the rest of your sponsorship budget. If one anchor sponsor and two $2,500 sponsors are secured, then only ten at $1,000 are needed to reach the sponsorship goal of $25,000 in our sample budget. Chapter 6 treats seeking sponsorships in more detail.

Another way to plug the gap in a budget is to use a "value-added" activity, such as an auction. Live auctions generally work best, with many high-ticket items available such as vacations, large meals prepared by local chefs in the winners' homes, art-

Is THE cost of the ticket or the auction bid considered a charitable donation?

In the past, donors could deduct the amount of the ticket price that was above the value of the event. You would assign a dollar value to the event to subtract from the ticket price with the remainder being the deductible portion. For instance, if your event was a golf outing, and the price to play was $100, the value would have been the going rate to play in your community plus the costs of perks such as meals and gifts. The remainder (if there was remaining value) would have been the portion of the cost that was tax deductible. If your event cost $1,000 per ticket for a meal worth $100, your deductible portion would have been $900.

Auction bids are generally not considered tax deductible because in most cases it is hard to determine the fair market value of a donated item.

Tax laws have changed recently, so research the existing laws and provide general guidelines about donations. Inform your guests what portion is tax deductible for their tax purposes. Always refer donors to their tax advisors for recommendations about deductibility.

work, wine, and jewelry. One event offered ten meals cooked in donors' homes for twelve guests by local chefs. Each meal sold for between $750 and $3,000, raising an additional $20,000 from the auction alone. (This assumes that the chefs have donated their services and food costs. Many chefs will do this to promote their talents and/or restaurants.)

I've found that professional auctioneers are comfortable being asked to donate their services for charity and do a wonderful job of moving you toward your goal. Stay away from silent auctions or Chinese auctions. I think they tend to clutter the look of the event and distract from the big-ticket items. Be cautious about offering too many low-value items. Chapter 12 describes how to design a successful auction.

Let's get started! Enter your known costs first. Research your unknown costs and enter them into the following chart. Then add in the profit needed to reach your goal. Now you have your fundraising goal. Start playing around with ticket costs and sponsor levels until you reach a balanced, achievable budget that will reach it!

With your budget set, your next step is to track expenses and income, comparing those to your budgeted amounts. Adjust your budget if necessary to keep your final goal attainable. This may mean adjusting costs if sponsorships aren't coming in as planned, or raising prices to attain your goal. Keep the committee apprised of how things are going with a financial report at each meeting. As you craft a plan to execute the fundraiser and begin to solicit sponsorships, your next step is to let the community know what's coming and how they can be a part of your event.

SUMMARY

1. Detail all anticipated expenses on an Excel spreadsheet.
2. Determine your fundraising goal and add it to your expense.
3. Determine your ticket price.
4. Identify what your sponsorship needs are to reach your fundraising goal.
5. Craft a message that will appeal to sponsors and approach them early, at least six months before the event. Some corporations set their charitable and marketing budgets a year in advance.
6. Keep accurate records and monitor your actual costs and income.
7. Keep your committee apprised of your progress.

	BUDGET	ACTUAL	VARIANCE
REVENUE			
Sponsorships			
Ticket sales			
Merchandise sales (T-shirts, etc)			
Beer and wine sales			
Registrations			
Partners' contributions			
Auction or other add on			
Donations			
Total Gross Revenue			
EXPENSES			
Food/Catering (cost per person/total)			
Rentals			
Tables			
Chairs			
Linen			
Tent and rentals			
Sound system			
Service			
Permits (event, alcohol, etc.)			
Alcohol			
Decorations			
Entertainment			
Awards			
Printing (invitations, programs)			
Credit card fees			
Photographer			
Supplies			
Insurance			
Total Costs			
NET PROCEEDS			
(total gross revenue minus total cost)			

CHAPTER FIVE

Invite Them and They Will Come

MARKETING

SPECIAL EVENTS put the "fun" in fundraising! Once you've identified your rationale for holding a fundraiser, clearly articulated the impact the funds raised will have on the community, assembled a dynamite committee, and crafted a realistic budget, then issuing the invitation is easy. Now you are bringing people together to have fun and support your cause. Guests might buy a ticket for $100 to a fancy dinner event, but if they know that their money is also feeding hungry people in their community, it's a win–win!

The first step is to craft a powerful message about your event. Emphasize its potential for positive effect on an issue or problem and how it will benefit the people in your community. Be honest and clear in your message. Tell why the money is needed and who is affected, giving specifics and issuing a call to action: "In this community, 30 percent of our children go hungry. You are invited to help make a difference by attending Bounty on the

Bricks." Next, identify who are the potential markets for your event. If it's a race, look for runners; if an auction, look for people who enjoy competitive bidding and have money to spend. Next, think about what other groups might be interested: Are there less obvious audiences? For instance, if your race is raising money for food pantries, consider who else supports food pantries. Congregations in your community, local businesses, and schools want to support local feeding efforts. If running in the race isn't an option, could donors walk? Volunteer? Sponsor? Let them know how to sign up, buy a ticket, or volunteer. When listing possible audiences, think creatively, beyond the obvious. Don't forget friends, colleagues, and families of committee members.

Having the right committee in place can answer many of your marketing challenges. Think back to the ticket-selling example in chapter 4. If ten committee members each sell twenty tickets, that's two hundred tickets! You can "sell out" the event before tickets even officially go on sale. If you're lucky enough to be in this situation, it's a good idea to hold back some tickets for general sale or for special guests who may want to attend. Holding back tickets will also avoid the perception that your event is only for "those with connections."

Once the audiences have been identified and the message or messages are completed (you may use a slightly different approach for each potential market), you'll be ready to develop a strategy to deliver them. Most likely you will approach each audience differently. Committee members might agree to call or email their friends and family. Runners might get the word through a local runners' newsletter or bulletin board. The following sample marketing plan may help you to craft your own strategy. Put dates in the planner for when messages will be released and indicate what media or avenues are best to send them through.

Graphics provide your event and organization with an identity. Used year after year, a graphic becomes a symbol that the community quickly associates with your event. Many nonprofits

March 1	Messages developed Graphics developed Marketing plan developed	All Digital
April 1	Teaser email/save the date If print invitation-design	Print or electronic
May 1	Media release Hire photographer Design poster Print invitation	Print, radio, and social media, word of mouth, etc. Print or digital
June 1	Ticket release Evite release Mail print invitation Poster	Print, radio and social media and others Email, social media Select venues
July 1	Auction Ticket sales press release Invite media to event	Website All media
August Event	Video, photograph Information on cause	Social, print, and broadcast media
September 1	Press release about success	All media

have access to an artist or designer who will develop the graphics and logos for the event. Waiving the fee is a nice way for an artist to donate to your cause. If you can't find a graphic designer to donate services, it may be worth putting money into your budget to pay someone. Look for someone whose style sends the message you want for your event. An amateur design will usually not reflect well on its quality. The message and images associated with your fundraiser are one factor your potential donors will evaluate to decide if the event is for them.

In my small community, the best way to market an event is by word of mouth. So having a well-connected committee is a huge asset when it comes to selling tickets. Each committee person is asked to commit to selling ten tickets. If you have ten committee members, that's one hundred tickets. Most people

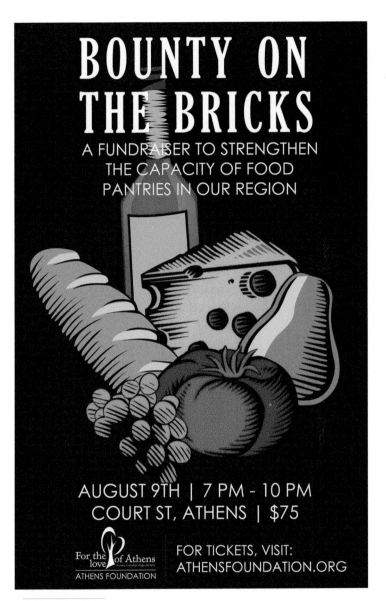

BOUNTY ON THE BRICKS

A FUNDRAISER TO STRENGTHEN THE CAPACITY OF FOOD PANTRIES IN OUR REGION

AUGUST 9TH | 7 PM - 10 PM
COURT ST, ATHENS | $75

For the love of Athens
in every township village and farm
ATHENS FOUNDATION

FOR TICKETS, VISIT:
ATHENSFOUNDATION.ORG

Poster artwork creates the "look" for the event.
Design by Lindsey Siegrist

will buy two, which easily gets your number to two hundred tickets. Promise sponsors a seat at the table, and you can easily sell one hundred more tickets. (We have been successful offering to hold tickets for a sponsor to purchase at an often sold-out event.) Invite your board members to buy a table for themselves and their clients or friends. You can reach your goal of four hundred guests fairly quickly if your message reaches the right people, your committee and board are involved in promoting the event, and you have a catchy graphic.

If your event is new, you may consider sending a "Save the Date" postcard or email announcements about six months prior to the event. Not only will this alert friends, donors, and guests that something new is coming, it will also inform other nonprofits that you have secured a date for your event. Just as others will pay attention to your event date, it's important to be aware of the schedule of other events in your community. The best way to dilute your effectiveness is to compete for guests with other nonprofits who have fundraisers on the same night as yours, or to schedule your benefit for the same day a football game, concert, festival, or other big community event is to be held. Most communities keep a calendar of events online; these may also be found at convention and visitors' centers, the chamber of commerce, or public libraries. Add your date to these calendars early.

If your event is fairly formal, a professionally designed invitation printed on quality paper with a return envelope is required, especially if your guests are over fifty years of age. While the under-fifty crowd will respond to a social media invitation, don't count on your older guests to use social media. Millennials may not RSVP at all, unless there are limited seats, making event planning difficult. If you need a head count, you will need to require an RSVP. Send the invitation two months to six weeks prior to the event. Most people are busy; giving guests enough time to include your fundraiser on their calendar will help boost success.

Save-the-date postcard helps guests plan for the date.
Courtesy of Athens Foundation

Whichever method you choose, include answers to the following questions: Who is holding the event? What is it? Why are you holding this event? When and where will the event be held? How do guests buy tickets and how much do they cost? Let guests know who you are and who your sponsors are: many people will respond if they see a familiar name or company. If a printed invitation is used, include a reply card with room for credit card information, meal preferences, guests' names, and any other necessary information. If you are using an online registration system, you'll need to find a way to collect this same information. This is a good opportunity to capture email and street addresses for thank-you notes to be sent after the event and for future invitations and solicitations.

Evite programs are useful for managing a fundraiser. Constant Contact is one low-cost marketing service used by numerous nonprofits, but there are many others. These programs offer design templates and flexible registration platforms that capture the information you need. They also give you the ability to easily email your guests with follow-up information, if necessary. Evite programs can process payments with credit cards as well, but shop for fees because a wide range is offered.

I don't recommend more traditional forms of marketing for fundraising events unless you are going for a very large, non-specific audience. Ads placed in a newspaper or on TV are very expensive; besides, most donors don't respond to these kinds of shotgun approaches. The more personal the invitation is, the more likely you'll reach your goal. For free coverage of your event, issue a press release sharing the story of what you are doing and why. Make plans that will allow you to share the success and impact of your fundraiser with the community by inviting the media or a photographer from the local paper to it. After the event, let your community know how much money you raised and how it will be used.

Sponsors will expect visibility for their contributions. Their company names and logos can be listed on the invitations and displayed at the event. We have used posters, banners, and place cards to recognize sponsors. Corporations will take their sponsorship gifts out of one of two budgets: marketing or charitable. If the gift is from the charitable budget, a prominent mention of a corporation's name is sufficient. If you are given marketing money, you may be asked to work with the marketing department to craft the visibility and message the company desires for its investment. If possible, incorporate a sponsor's product into your event. A race could hand out cups or T-shirts with the sponsor logos included. There is, however, a fine line between mounting a fabulous event and being overrun by sponsor messaging. Keep it subtle.

These events are an excellent opportunity to cultivate larger donors. Ask one of your board members to invite someone you hope will eventually make a larger gift to the organization. Bringing prospects "into the family" gives them a sense of belonging to your cause. It also provides an opportunity to get to know them better and build trust. Similarly, you might want to invite local officials, legislators, or other VIPs who could be cultivated to support your cause. Elected officials pay for their own tickets or entry to avoid excessive-gifting regulations.

A fundraising event also offers a great opportunity for people who attend to learn about your organization! Don't overwhelm your guests, but a tasteful information piece or very short, but professionally produced, video might invite them to view your website or attend a future program. These events are gateway vehicles for new donors; you don't want to miss an opportunity to share and collect information.

Capture the event! Hire a professional photographer and/or videographer. You could even use a drone to secure an aerial shot of an outdoor event. You'll be able to use these images on

Quality photos taken by professional photographers help promote future events.
Photo courtesy of Dan Kubus

your website and in your annual report as well as for marketing next year's fundraiser.

Your final marketing pieces are thank-you notes or letters and a press release sharing the story of your success and impact on the community. Committee members should be invited to help with the thank-you letters by signing or writing notes to donors and guests. Everyone who contributed should be thanked: guests, sponsors, in-kind donors, volunteers, and media—anyone who made your event a success. The final press release will recap what you intended to do, summarize your results, name all those who made it possible, and thank the community. A key marketing tool is the "thank you"; you can't do it too much or overlook it. Donors and volunteers will remember your thoughtfulness. When you give the money raised to the designated charity, seize the opportunity for a "big check" photo.

Reaching your fundraising goal may depend on the effectiveness of your marketing campaign, so put your best foot forward! Good marketing will boost attendance at future fundraisers and strengthen your relationship with donors. It will tell your story, letting the community know who you are and what you care about.

SUMMARY

1. Identify all your potential markets, participants, and audiences.
2. Craft a message or messages that will relate to each market. The message should be clear and compelling and include a call to action.
3. Develop graphics to communicate the message about your event that speaks to potential audiences as well as reflects the flavor of your event.
4. Develop a timeline and vehicle for releasing messages to each market. These should include press releases, invitations, social media, verbal communications, personal letters, and photography.
5. Include sponsor recognition in your messaging and carefully draft a plan to give sponsors the visibility and connection they are seeking with their contributions.
6. Ask committee and board members to share the message with friends.
7. Ask board members to invite key donor prospects to your event.
8. Tell your story, before, during, and after the event.
9. Celebrate your success through the media.
10. Thank everyone!

CHAPTER SIX

Cover the Basics

SPONSORS

OFFERING SPONSORSHIPS to local, regional, or national businesses is a great way to align your cause with like-minded business owners. It's also the best way to cover the cost of your event so that everything else—such as tickets, auctions, and fees —is profit. Start by considering what businesses care about your issue, organization, or event. If you are holding a race, then stores that feature running-shoe or sporting-goods manufacturers would see the benefit of sponsoring your event. If you're raising money to feed hungry people, go to your local grocery. Look where you spend money as an organization. For instance, if you do all your printing at local vendors, they might be willing to give back with cash or in-kind donations. Look at your committee for connections. If a committee member owns a business or works for a larger corporation, ask that member to seek corporate support. Next, look where there is money in the community. Find the person with the closest connection to approach this sponsor. This could be a member of your committee or board of directors who has a personal relationship with the donor or business.

I have failed miserably in seeking sponsors when I asked a volunteer to make a cold call, without first researching what the company cares about and who its market is. In addition, consider how hard businesses work to distinguish themselves from competitors. For instance, a local bank may be proud of the fact that it remains locally owned and run and, thereby, can be more nimble in business transactions than the international bank around the corner. Be sensitive to how businesses want to position themselves. Don't ask major competitors to share space in your program—especially on the same page! Some businesses will even stipulate that they will only help if their competitor is not approached.

Once you've identified potential sponsors, spend some time researching and thinking about what is the appropriate amount to request. You can find information about their history of giving by asking someone connected to the business or a nonprofit that has received support from the company in the past. Look at the gift levels they've made in your community. If it's a large company, look on its website to see what kinds of causes and organizations the company has supported. It's often helpful to talk with your board or committee about what is the right amount to ask for. Remember the story, "Goldilocks and the Three Bears"? You're looking for the amount that is "just right."

A word about asking: many volunteers will join a committee with the clear message, "I'll help you in any way I can, but don't ask me to raise money." A little coaching and, even, role-playing could help in this situation. Have one person represent the business prospect and another do the asking. Have the committee give feedback to build awareness and comfort about going out and asking. Go in teams of two. Businesses are often looking for ways to spread the word about their product. Associating with an event that has a good reputation and is raising money to give back to the community, help a good cause, or improve lives is an attractive proposition to them. Some larger companies even have marketing dollars set aside to increase their brand visibility and consider giving back to the community as part of their strategy. Go into an "ask" confident that you have something of value to offer them.

Corporate giving has changed in the last twenty years. Many national firms have limited their sponsorship dollars to organizations in their "home" communities and those causes for which their employees volunteer. Without a personal connection or a highly visible national event, you're not likely to succeed in landing a national sponsor.

The next step in preparing to solicit a business is writing a proposal. This should be a short summary of your project that includes the amount you are seeking, the perks you are offering to sponsors, and your total goal. Use clear, concise, and direct language. Keep it to one page. If you have graphics, use them. Tailor each request to a specific business. You could include a pledge form that serves to commit on paper the terms of the agreement between you and the sponsor.

Now it's time to make the ask. Generally, a letter sent without a personal visit will yield far less in contributions. If you use a board member to make the connection or appointment, make sure they are included in the call along with the appropriate committee member, chair, other board member, or CEO. Bring your written proposal. Then start the conversation. Listen carefully to what potential donors are telling you. They may say their passion is supporting education in the region. If you're asking them to sponsor a race for breast cancer, they may not be interested. You can thank them for sharing a little more about what they care about and exit. If you sense they are open to your cause, state clearly and upfront what you are asking, the amount you are seeking, and how the company will benefit. Many organizations

One sponsor's product was used to create a centerpiece.
Photo courtesy of Ben Siegel

will develop a table of sponsor benefits. These include use of company logos on merchandise or displays at the event, access to the event or free admission for the company's owners or staff, products to be used at the event, and advertising space in the event program.

One of our local sponsors manufactures shoes and boots. Since its sponsorship was the lead gift, we decided to feature its product as a part of the table decorations. The company donated a box of children's western-style boots, and the creative decorating crew turned them into flowerpots!

A word of caution: don't give away the store. Provide as many perks as you can but don't offer those that will cost you money and diminish your profits. Don't leave the solicitation request form on their desks and say you'll get back with them later. Later will never come. Close the deal before you leave their offices.

A WORD ON thanking donors and sponsors: Your sponsors are getting something in return for their help. Whether it's visibility, tickets, or the goodwill gained from association with your organization's cause or name, they will be receiving something of value. Be careful not to overdo your thanks with lavish gifts. It's okay to give gifts, but keep their value minimal. Receiving an expensive gift from a nonprofit will, at the least, make donors uncomfortable. At the worst, it will make them angry that you have wasted your profits on them. So give wisely.

During visits to potential sponsors, have your board member share briefly why he or she is committed to this project, what it involves, and what is being asked of the donor. Be specific in your ask. Don't merely present each donor with a menu of levels of giving. You are targeting these people for a reason: you know their ability to give and an appropriate amount to ask for that matches your needs. So go ahead and ask. Present your case concisely; ask for the support; then take a breath. Allow time for sponsors to ask questions, consider your request, and respond. Don't fill the empty space with babble. Sit quietly and wait. They may agree to everything you've presented. Great! Pat yourself on the back after you have them sign a promise or pledge detailing how much they will give, when the money is due, how they would like to pay and be recognized, and what benefits they will receive for their donation. Thank them and leave. Or, they may say, "not at this time." Again, thank them and follow up. Keep them informed about your event and its success. Ask again next year.

When you get back to the office, copy the contract and mail it with an invoice and a thank-you letter to the sponsor. If you need graphic files or product from the sponsor for your event, ask how you can receive these. Thanking donors is the most important step in any fundraising.

Next, follow through with your promises. If you promised tickets, put them in the mail. If you guaranteed visibility, send donors copies of your program, invitation, news articles, or any other piece that mentions their company's name. Your thoroughness and professionalism will make the next time you request a meeting for support a lot easier to secure. Once the relationship is established and solidified with follow-throughs, you are assured a loyal donor.

SAMPLE PROPOSAL

From (*name of organization*)
For (*name of event*) Sponsorship
Date of event
Time of event
Amount requested: $

You have been a valued partner in our efforts to support (*your cause*) in our region. We are happy to announce the work will continue! The board of directors of the (*your organization*) asks (*xyz business*) consideration of support for the (*name of event*) event. With your sponsorship, we will reach our goal of $(*xyz*) which will hopefully leverage $(*xyz*) additional dollars for (*your cause*).

As a sponsor, your logo and name will appear on the invitation, evite, newsletter, and program. (*You might indicate how many people will attend.*) We anticipate the same huge success and early sell out.

As a result of last year's event, (*give detail of your past success*).

(Add a paragraph about your cause and why funds are needed.)

(Summarize the event in one paragraph: what will happen and when, and who will attend.)

Thank you for your consideration of our request!

Sincerely,

Jane Doe
Executive Director

SUMMARY

1. Determine the level of total sponsorship dollars your event needs to be successful.

2. Develop a one-page summary detailing how sponsors will benefit. This could include the number of times each will be named, the visibility of a sponsor's logo on displays, merchandise, and programs, and the number of tickets and tables each will receive.

3. Identify potential sponsors by talking with your committee and board about whom they know and who has an affiliation with your cause or event.

4. Ask a friend or colleague of a potential sponsor to make the appointment.

5. Share why you care about this issue or event, what the event is, and how the sponsor can help.

6. Sit quietly and wait for the response!

7. Follow up immediately with a contract, an invoice, and a thank-you letter.

8. Follow through on your promises to the sponsor.

9. Share the results of your event with your sponsor.

CHAPTER SEVEN

Don't Dance Alone

PARTNERSHIPS

ONE WAY to greatly increase your impact is to look at who else cares about your cause. Are there funders who are investing in the same cause who could boost your net profits and magnify their investments at the same time? Strong sponsors and partners are what make events super profitable. Sponsorships are needed to cover the costs associated with the event. And funding partners help to supersize the outcome.

Funding collaborations are a delicate dance. Relationships and trust are built over time. Each partner gives a little, then evaluates the outcomes. If the collaboration is a success, partners are usually open to future collaboration. A clear understanding of what your organization's priorities are and where those priorities overlap with other organizations or funders is the key to entering into any collaboration. In our case, enlisting the support of two other foundations continued a conversation and collaboration that had started over ten years ago. I met the other two foundation directors at our state philanthropy conference. They both funded in my area, but were located in other parts of the state. They were looking for a partner on the ground who understood the community. Both women became valued colleagues and treasured friends.

You can find partners in several ways. Looking at who donates money in your region is the perfect place to start. A search on Guidestar or the Foundation Center will help access the information you need. You may already work with these organizations or funders. Next look at your cause. If your fundraiser is for breast cancer research, would a foundation or drug company that donates to breast cancer research match what you raise? Again, these online services will help provide more detailed information on funders' priorities. For our event, we were raising money to feed hungry people. We were already involved with two other foundations in this work. Their decision to help with our fundraiser was a natural extension of an ongoing relationship.

Our two partners were the Sisters Health Foundation and the Osteopathic Heritage Foundation of Nelsonville. With their support, we decided to move forward with Bounty on the Bricks.

After partnering on this project for four years, I called Cynthia Drennan, retired CEO of Sisters Health Foundation, and Terri Donlin Huesman, president of the Osteopathic Heritage Foundation, and asked why they do this work and, in particular, what are their goals in collaborating on this event? Cynthia said, "From the beginning, (we want) to acknowledge the large serious need (for food). None of us alone can address this problem successfully. So we need to work together with others. I support collaboration. We ask for it from our grantees, and it's a simple way for us to model what we recommend. Then there's efficiency: why should we have three different (grants) processes when we can work together and have one? We have a collective intention to help individual food pantries to develop their capacity. That's why we've encouraged the individual pantries to join the food-

THE SISTERS Health Foundation is guided by its vision of "healthy people in healthy communities" with special concern for people who are poor or otherwise underserved, including increasing access to healthy foods.

The Osteopathic Heritage Foundation of Nelsonville exists to improve the health and quality of life in the community through education, research, and service consistent with osteopathic heritage.

bank. And we want to commonly support the foodbank to do its job."

Finally, I asked her how she benefits from the partnership. "I have partners out there! I have someone to talk to and brainstorm with. Personally, I rely on you to be able to talk and learn together. We're not all at that same level (when talking about foundations' collaborating); some of us have been with this a while. We've learned that we need others we can trust and have a willingness to work together."

Terri shared, "One of the core values of our approach to grant making is partnerships and recognizing the value of local organizations and their expertise and knowledge about the community we're serving. We view the Athens County Foundation as a trusted and valued resource. Having the ACF as lead local agency provides a level of trust that the fundraiser and grants program will be executed at the highest level with integrity and the right strategies.

"Access to healthy foods has been our funding priority since 2003. Supporting the foodbank and the food pantry network is the front door to healthy foods. It's a strategy that needs to be addressed."

I asked how this partnership furthers their work at the OHFN. She responded, "One of our core values is advancing our mission through partnership and collaboration. We aren't physically located in the region and have a small staff. This partnership enables expansion of our reach and supports more organizations than we could on our own. We do better when we work together."

I asked them both, "What have we learned over the last three years?" "How hard collaboration is!" Terri responded. "It takes time to develop this level of trust and collaboration. You can't overestimate how important time sitting across the table from one another and breaking bread is. Getting to know each other as individuals was important to us personally and translated to our trust between the organizations."

How do you find good partners? Start by looking at funders you already have a relationship with. Talk to their program officers about your upcoming event and gauge their interest in helping. If you don't have a relationship, you'll need a good amount of lead time, probably at least a year, to start to form one. Try to get an appointment with foundations and share who you are and some of your goals. Ask how they work and what their priorities are. If you see a path forward, indicated by some overlap in your priorities and theirs, develop a proposal for these organizations detailing the opportunity to partner on your fundraiser. Include what role each entity will play and what the responsibilities and obligations are of each. If they aren't interested in your event, you've still begun a conversation that may bear fruit later on.

Partners are not sponsors. Their money doesn't cover the cost of your event. Their funds match what you raise, then all of the money goes toward your charitable cause.

If you are fortunate to find partners in your work, a written agreement is required. Collaboration is tricky and having everyone's expectations spelled out in writing, confirmed, and signed will assure a strong relationship and lessen the potential for disagreements and disappointment. Partners should be treated differently than sponsors. Their support will most likely be more

Event partners present the "big check" to the SEO Foodbank. Shown (*left to right*) are representatives of the Osteopathic Heritage Foundation of Nelsonville and the Sisters Health Foundation, the Foodbank director, and a representative of the Athens County Foundation.
Photo courtesy of Athens County Foundation

significant, so they may appreciate your sharing more detail about their organizations or foundations with your donors and guests. They may want seats on the planning committee and will most likely attend the event. They will definitely want to be present at the "big check" event when you distribute the earnings of the fundraiser and the partner's funds to your worthy cause. If the event is a fundraiser for your organization, you should plan a "big check" event for yourself.

Again, thank your partners profusely! They are invaluable collaborators in your work. Let them know it!

SUMMARY

1. Look at your existing relationships with funders. Are there possible partners among them?

2. Make an appointment to share your project and determine their interest.
3. If you have no relationships, look at who funds in your area by examining the websites of other nonprofits. You can also look at the foundation center website at www .foundationcenter.org to research who funds in your area or discipline.
4. Make an appointment to begin a conversation with the new potential funder about your organization, cause, and event.
5. If you find a collaborating partner, develop a shared agreement that can be signed and followed to guide the collaboration.
6. Keep partners involved and informed every step of the way.
7. Include partners in the event and give them visibility.
8. Include partners in the "big check" event.
9. Continue the conversation; it may lead to further collaborations.

CHAPTER EIGHT

What's the Plan?

LOGISTICS

Most questions that begin with "how, what, and where" fall under the umbrella of logistics. How much room will we need? What permits are required? Where is the water? Where are the electrical outlets? How will waste be handled? What regulations need our attention? What resources do we need to find? When do we set up; what is our sequencing? What supplies and equipment need to be ordered? Where will we park our cars and our trucks? Where do we place our staging areas? Do we need security or insurance riders? What happens if it rains? Answering these questions is the job for the detail-oriented, systematic thinkers in your group.

You'll know you've got the right person for the job when he or she pulls out the Excel charts. A good logistics plan has a list of everything that needs to happen leading up to, during, and after the event. There are dates, times, and responsibilities attached to each task. Details are included with contact information, phone numbers, company names, and addresses. This comes in handy if, for example, the sound company is running late, or you're ready to pay a vendor and need an address. This is not a task for the intuitive members of your team. It's where the strategic thinkers shine.

Start with a map or blueprint and an Excel spreadsheet. First, decide where your event will take place and whose permission you need to use that space. Next, map out the dimensions or route of the event. If it's a race, include detailed information about trails, roads, paths, bathrooms, and parking. If it's a gala, draw out the ballroom and place the dance floor, tables and chairs, bars, coat rack, and parking, indicating clearly where you want them on that map. If the true measurements of your space aren't readily available from the venue, find a measuring wheel to walk the space yourself and record the measurements on your sketch. This is not an area where you want to trust your intuition. Real numbers will guarantee success—or at least enough space for all your tables and chairs! If your event has a designated rain location, you will need two drawings: one for each space. The details should include the seating arrangement, showing the placement and size of the tables and the number of chairs at each; the locations for serving food and drinks, as well as the bussing stations for clearing tables, and the trash containers. Also include the placement of amenities, such as a check-in area, restrooms, and the entertainment stages. (Some people love graph paper for this job.) You'll probably need this map if you are applying for a liquor license or working with a rental hall. Outdoor events will need a similar map.

Ask a person in the know about what permits you will need. City or county permit offices will be able to give you the correct information. Some permits take a while to obtain because the applications may need to go through committees or hearings before final approvals are granted. So start early, six to nine months ahead of the event. Permits that you might need include: permission to close or temporarily block streets and occupancy, alcohol or gaming, and parking permits.

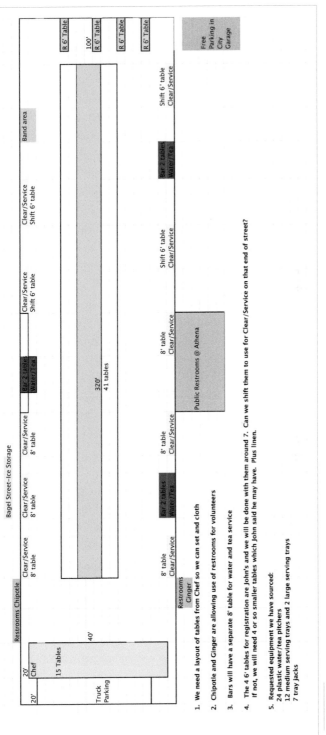

Restrooms Chipotle

Bagel Street--Ice Storage

20'

20' Chef

Truck Parking

15 Tables

40'

Band area

Clear/Service
8' table

Clear/Service
8' table

Clear/Service
8' table

Bar 2 tables
Water/Tea

Clear/Service
8' table

Clear/Service
Shift 6' table

Clear/Service
Shift 6' table

320'
41 tables

R 6' Table

100'
R 6' Table

R 6' Table

R 6' Table

Restrooms
Ginger

8' table
Clear/Service

Bar 2 tables
Water/Tea

8' table
Clear/Service

8' table
Clear/Service

Public Restrooms @ Athena

Shift 6' table
Clear/Service

Shift 6' table
Clear/Service

Bar 2 tables
Water/Tea

Shift 6' table
Clear/Service

Free Parking in City Garage

1. We need a layout of tables from Chef so we can set and cloth

2. Chipotle and Ginger are allowing use of restrooms for volunteers

3. Bars will have a separate 8' table for water and tea service

4. The 4 6' tables for registration are John's and we will be done with them around 7. Can we shift them to use for Clear/Service on that end of street?
   If not, we will need 4 or so smaller tables which John said he may have. Plus linen.

5. Requested equipment we have sourced:
   24 plastic water/tea pitchers
   12 medium serving trays and 2 large serving trays
   7 tray jacks

The placements and sizes of tables and bars for an event held in a mall are precisely shown on graph paper.

Make friends with your fire chief! Any large gathering of people usually involves the fire department, which has regulations you will need to follow. Invite a representative or the fire marshal to walk through your plan and venue with you to make sure all regulations are followed and that you understand what is necessary to make the event safe. For instance, candles are usually a concern and, therefore, are highly regulated. Occupancy numbers fall under the fire regulations. If your event is outside, then allowing for a "fire lane," or easy access to the site, will be required to protect the safety of your guests.

I have worked with extremely logistical thinkers. The first year of an event, the committee had designed a rustic theme with burlap and hay bales. The morning of the fundraiser we all met early to start to set up. A pickup truck arrived with the hay bales that were to become seats during the cocktail hour. We transformed the street into a country picnic! Then, around noon the fire marshal walked through the area. He commanded us to get rid of the hay bales and all unnecessary burlap. He said we couldn't use candles, and all forty tables needed to be moved three feet west. I was grateful for our logistics' team; they handled the demands with a smile, readjusting their plans along the way. And, as you might expect, the guests never knew how many last minute changes occurred.

Make friends with your health inspector. Serving food requires extra caution to prevent harming your guests. Adequate water for hand washing and food prep will be necessary. Hot food needs to stay at a proper temperature; so does cold food. If your event is outside, use a "hot" truck or hot boxes and a "cold" truck, all specially designed to meet these requirements. It is the responsibility of the chefs and caterers to meet food-service regulations, but be aware of this requirement.

Electricity is crucial at any event. Your map should show the locations of all outlets and what their capacity is. Even a golf tournament will probably need a microphone and a way to keep

Southeast Ohio Foodbank loans hot and cold trucks from its Meals on Wheels program to caterers for an event.
Photo courtesy of Jo Carpenter

beer cold! Check with all your vendors: those supplying food, entertainment, and decorations. Make sure each has access to the right amount of power (110 or 220 volts), and that all cords are provided to meet power needs. You'll also need to have mats or other ways to cover cords so your guests don't trip on them!

If you choose to serve alcohol at your event, you'll need to check your state requirements. Permits may take several months to gain approval. You will need a copy of the license before you order alcohol from your wholesaler. Each state will have its own regulations. (For example, in Ohio, wholesalers are not permitted to donate alcohol, unless you are selling it at auction.) Whether you serve alcohol or not, check with your insurance agent about the need for additional liability coverage. Will you need extra security as well? You may be able to work with your local law enforcement, or you may need to hire security for your event. Some communities require an event license; some take a percentage of the ticket-price tax. Know what is required where you are.

Bar placement should be strategically planned to allow for your guests'
convenience. *Photo courtesy of Ben Siegel*

Donated flowers and bread create a pleasing table set up.
Photo courtesy of Ben Siegel

Flowers donated from neighborhood gardens were used for displays.
Photo courtesy of Jo Carpenter

To set up a bar you'll probably need ice, corkscrews and bottle openers, and a place to display what drinks are available with their prices—if you plan to charge for drinks. Allow enough bars so that guests don't have to wait too long in line for a drink.

Decorations depend on the type of event. Again, most of these items can be donated or bought at low cost. Less is sometimes better. Keep "line of sight" free at dinner tables so guests can talk easily with each other. Skirt tables with tablecloths. Fresh flowers can add a lot to any event.

We are becoming much more aware of the impact of waste on our quality of life and sustainability as a community. The waste produced at your event needs careful consideration. Recycle what you can; take care to choose materials that can be recycled,

A Rural Action Zero Waste Program managed all waste products, including food, glass, plastic, and paper. *Photo courtesy of Ben Siegel*

reused, or composted. In our area, thanks to a local nonprofit Rural Action devoted to sustainability, we strive for a zero-waste event. The nonprofit provides volunteers to sort trash at the end of the evening and route each type of trash to be recycled or composted.

Parking is important to your guests. Secure permission to use any parking lots, meters, or open fields that you might need. Some events offer valet services to guests. If those services are not offered, alert your guests to where they can park, how far they will need to walk, and what the parking will cost, if applicable. Some guests will need handicap accessible parking and an easy, obstacle-free route to the event, so include that information, too.

You may have other vehicles to coordinate as well. Food vendors or entertainers may have trucks that need to be stored somewhere. Keep in mind that permissions are usually necessary for special parking spaces, and, in the case of food trucks or carts, available parking close to a power source is required. Traffic flow is another consideration, especially at an outdoor event. Your goal

The bars, bus stations, high tops, and tables used in this event came from a rental company and local donations. *Photo courtesy of Dan Kubus*

is to make access easy and to keep your guests' comfort and safety foremost in your planning.

Most events will need some equipment that you don't have. Party rental companies can handle most event needs. Carefully consider what you will need to rent, what the costs are, and whether the company will deliver, and if setup is required. Do you know someone who would donate what you need?

If you will invite dancing at your event, make sure a dance floor is available, either through your venue or from a rental agency. The band or speakers will most likely need amplification and a sound person to control volumes. Have the sound person visit the space ahead of time so he or she is aware of the requirements of the space. This will assure that the sound will reach all your guests. If the company charges, include its fee and any rentals that are needed in your budget. On the day of the event, run a sound check to assure everything is working properly.

Since the comfort of your guests is your top concern, plan carefully for those who need special provisions. Is your space wheelchair accessible? Are amplification, earphones, or signing available for the hearing-impaired guests? Is the lighting sufficient for elderly or sight-impaired guests? A little extra thought will guarantee a more positive experience for everyone.

Check out the restrooms. Are facilities on hand, or will you need to make provisions? If the event is outside, there may be a facility nearby that you can request access to for the period of your event. If there isn't, you will need to rent facilities. Add this cost to your budget and don't forget to accommodate those with special needs.

You have probably guessed by now that a detailed timetable is a great tool to keep everyone on track. The first timeline you'll need is a month-by-month schedule of what is to be done. You may find an hour-by-hour sequencing useful on the days leading up to your event with specific individuals assigned to each duty. It will help your volunteers know exactly when they need to be where, doing what. Keep these records, maps, timelines, sources, and invoices; they will make your job next year so much easier! Here is a sample timeline.

SAMPLE TIMELINE

Nine months to one year out:	Confirm date
	Confirm committee chairs
	Develop sponsor list
	Set meeting schedule
	Confirm venue and rain location
Eight months out:	Confirm price
	Develop graphics and messages
	Develop marketing plan
	Draw up budget
	Add teams to committees

Seven months out:	Begin volunteer recruitment
	Develop website and prepare "save the date" invitations and emails
	Start applications for permits
	Develop sponsor list and materials
Six months out:	Begin sponsorship solicitation
	Begin auction solicitation
	Confirm permits
	Test evite
	Prepare media launch
	Confirm caterer
	Release the "save the date" materials
Five months out:	Confirm volunteer needs
	Confirm equipment needs
Four months out:	Hire musicians, auctioneers, and other entertainment
	Confirm decorations and setup
	Plan beverages
Three months out:	Open ticket sales
	Hire photographer
	Release media statements about your event
	Order supplies
Two months out:	Monitor ticket sales and messaging
One month out:	Confirm and finalize everything
Event:	Have fun!
One month after: (*tasks completed*)	Send all "thank yous"
	Hold a committee celebration
	Report all outcomes to sponsors, partners, guests, and the public
	Pay all bills and return equipment

The week leading up to the event, a detailed Excel spreadsheet can be a handy tool for mapping tasks, showing who is responsible and exactly when and where the task needs to occur. Share this information with key people and include contact names, numbers, and addresses for everyone!

Although the entire committee will help set up and tear down your event, the logistics chair is the overseer of these operations. Carefully consider the sequencing, need for volunteers, and the layout of the event. The logistics, event, or volunteer chairs could consider providing water and snacks for workers during setup or teardown.

SUMMARY

1. Start early—nine months to one year out.
2. Identify and secure site for your event.
3. Map out the event on paper.
4. Develop a month-by-month timeline.
5. Secure necessary permissions and permits.
6. List resources needed, their costs, and when and where you will secure them.
7. Add the resource-procurement detail to the timeline.
8. Share timelines with all subchairs, including a committee contact information sheet.
9. Supervise setup and teardown.

CHAPTER NINE

The Key to a Donor's Heart

FOOD AND BEVERAGES

THE OFFER of food always makes us feel welcome. Whether attending an ice cream social or a five-course gourmet meal, guests like food. We come together over food as families, friends, and community. If your event does not include a meal, your food and beverage needs are minimal. Usually snacks and drinks accompany non-meal events. If you are planning a golf tournament, you may provide golfers with a snack bag to take with them on the course and position coolers of beer and refreshments at select holes. But if you're serving a meal, you have many decisions to make. The easiest way to plan a meal is to hire a caterer. It's the most expensive way as well, but if your black-tie event requires that level of sophistication, include it in your budget. Most caterers charge a fixed fee per person. You can ask to see their menu suggestions, or come up with your own. I tend to trust the experts! For instance, when planning an annual meeting, the caterer suggested a five-ounce steak. Being a vegetarian, I couldn't

Chef Alfonso Constriciani
Photo courtesy of Joe Bell

believe that would be a popular selection. Imagine my surprise when over 75 percent of the guests chose the steak, thereby reminding me to trust the experts. Most chefs are very creative and know what's in season, what people like, what's trending, and how to craft magnificent menus at a decent price.

Using a professional also makes complying with health department regulations easier and assures that your guests will eat safe food. A professional will usually have the equipment needed to prepare the food, serving and kitchen staff on hand, and storage facilities. If your event is at a venue with a food service on site, you have it easy! If not, you may need to source all of this yourself, from serving dishes to hot plates and boxes. I don't recommend you plan an elaborate food event without a professional—a hired caterer or volunteer chef—to supervise everything related to food preparation and services.

Sign a contract with your caterer to protect both your interests. Clearly detail how many people will be served, how many courses are involved, what food will be served, how the caterer will be paid, and the deadlines for submitting menus and head counts. Many caterers may need to be paid a portion of the cost upfront or at the event.

These days many people have food restrictions, due to either medical or personal reasons. Having a detailed menu available ahead of time will help ward off a problem at the event. Some guests may want to know all the ingredients of a dish. You can be as accommodating as you choose, but chefs may change recipes or not disclose all ingredients. You can also list a disclaimer on your invitation stating you are not able to handle special diets at this event. It's up to you.

One year a guest complained to the chef that the green pepper in her meal contained gluten, and the person who ate the suspicious pepper was going into anaphylactic shock. After checking with both the chef and a local physician at the event, the food coordinator dismissed the complaint from the overanxious guest. No one died or even fell ill!

Add options to accommodate vegan guests: in this case, grain-stuffed peppers elegantly presented. *Photo courtesy of Joe Bell*

Events can be designed around food. Maybe a seasonal food, such as corn, could be the focus of an event and menu. In Athens, an entrepreneurial farmer who grows pawpaws (a tree fruit with a sweet, banana-like taste) started a fall-harvest festival. The event includes pawpaw beer and ice cream—even a cook-off! Families camp by the lake and enjoy a weekend of pawpaw fun.

Many local restaurants and individuals in your community are in the business of preparing food. For our event, we wanted to know that our chef partners had the ability to prepare large quantities of locally sourced, top-quality food and get it on the table in a fairly short period of time. That narrowed the list of chefs to a few of the more experienced ones used to catering to larger crowds.

Once your menu is decided, you'll have a good idea of what you'll need to set your table. You'll know how much service you'll need: what kind and size of plates, bowls, glasses, cups, and flat-ware. The venue of your event may determine whether you use fine china or a disposable product. For our outdoor event, we found bamboo dishes online that are compostable after use. While

MANY OF my events are planned around food. Beginning with our goal of feeding more people living in hunger, we decided to use locally sourced food and local chefs as our theme. Local sourcing is sometimes more expensive, but often provides a high value to both the guests and the local farmers. Local foods are an important part of our community, but, I wondered, why is local considered better? So I turned to the Internet.

Molly Watson on the website *About Food* says there are eight reasons to go local:

1. Local foods are fresher and taste better.
2. Local foods are seasonal.
3. Local foods usually have less negative environmental impact.
4. Local foods preserve green space and farmland.
5. Local foods promote food safety.
6. Local foods promote variety.
7. Local foods support your local economy.
8. Local foods create community. (This was music to my ears!)

There you have it: Food Creates Community!

it's debatable whether it is more "green" to compost or to wash china, I'd advise against using Styrofoam or other products that will go straight to the landfill after use.

Beverages may be handled by the caterer or separately. If caterers can take care of this aspect of your event, you will have a lot less work. They will have the liquor permit, equipment, and staff to serve your guests. Decide early on if alcohol will be served and budget for it. You can recoup some cost by charging for drinks, or give your guests drinks, or give them one or two drink tickets and have them purchase additional tickets.

If you run your own bar, find bartenders who know what they are doing. Inviting your kids' friends to tend bar can result in huge revenue loss from over-pours and the potential for alcohol abuse. Bartenders should be of age and know or be taught the proper drink size, how to mix drinks, and how to cut off alcohol abusers. Nothing ruins an event faster than a loud, drunk guest!

Nonalcoholic drinks are a necessity. Water should be offered at all events. Keep the sustainability of our earth in mind and avoid plastic bottles at all costs. Use nice pitchers of ice water at dinners and water stations at outdoor events with recyclable cups. Other choices might include iced tea, sports drinks, and lemonade. I would avoid soda for health reasons.

SUMMARY

1. Decide what food and beverages will complement your event.
2. Decide who will source and provide food.
3. Plan menus with your committee or a caterer and negotiate contracts with caterers.
4. Plan beverage options and order.
5. Plan pricing, if necessary.
6. Coordinate schedules for food delivery and service.
7. Communicate all food and beverage equipment needs and schedules to the logistics committee.
8. Provide the marketing committee with food and beverage details such as menus and prices.
9. Don't forget to offer something for vegetarians, nondrinkers, and others preferring alternative choices.
10. If you are not able to provide for individual food preferences, add a food disclaimer to marketing materials.

CHAPTER TEN

Keep Them Dancing

ENTERTAINMENT

MANY FUNDRAISERS feature some form of entertainment. The purpose of performers is to bring another layer or dimension to the experience for your guests. Remember, the more fun they are having, the more they will associate that feeling with your organization or cause, and the more they will give!

The event you plan will determine what type of entertainment is appropriate. Think about your guests: What would they enjoy? Is a dance band the ticket? Or a DJ? Where will they perform? How much space is available? Is there power available? Where do you even find a band, anyway? If you know any performers or musicians, invite them to serve on your committee and make one entertainment chair. He or she will already know most of the acts in town and will be in a much better position to negotiate fees and dates. If you can't find a musician to add to your committee, check with local venues for a list of local

A guest dances with a "Honey for the Heart" puppet.
Photo courtesy of Jo Carpenter

performers. Even restaurants that regularly hire performers can help provide names.

Someone on the committee should check the entertainment out. Go hear them play or perform or watch a video of the performers to get a sense of their act and its appropriateness for your event. This is also a chance to be creative. Musicians are popular, but what about a storyteller, dancers, magicians, or even a mime? We used a mime at an airport opening gala; it was great fun seeing him ride the escalator and interact with guests. Some theater companies can perform a short play or skit that could be tied to your event theme or cause. Film can be used if it relates to the cause and can be turned into a fundraising event. A screening of the film about hunger in the US, *A Seat at the Table*, generated rich conversation in our community and increased support for the event.

Mengyuan Yuan and Debra Rentz perform opera arias.
Photo courtesy of Ben Siegel

Comedians could present material relevant to your cause or organization. Avoid any acts that could be offensive to your guests, though. I've used cartoonists as a fundraising add-on to draw guests. If dancing is the focus, a DJ can bring a wide variety of sounds to your event and will, most likely, cost less than a full band. Generally, performers are not free unless they believe in your cause. Then they may be willing to donate their services to you. (You can capture the value of this donation as an in-kind donation, offer them a receipt for their tax purposes, and add them to your donor list!) Some performers are bound by union-membership requirements as to what they can do without receiving payment. If you have a donor willing to sponsor entertainment, you might be able to bring in a big name. At the airport-opening gala, our committee chair loved Cajun music and sponsored Beau-Soleil, a nationally known band from Louisiana. Guests danced on the concourse till late in the evening!

Most performers will require some sort of sound system—a simple amplifier that they haul in themselves or an elaborate setup of speakers, wireless mics, and mixing board. Know when

Performers Morgan Hager and Ry Burhans entertain guests.
Photo courtesy of Dan Kubus

you need to call in a professional. The performer may tell you who to hire to do the job. Outdoor spaces are especially hard to manage. Sound tends to be aimed in one direction and dissipates the further from its source, although speakers can be placed strategically to correct this. The other factor to consider when planning sound is the audience. Human bodies absorb sound; what seems loud at sound check can disappear at the event. For instance, at an indoor event held in a mall, we hired an opera quartet. At rehearsal in the empty promenade, the sound blasted through the space. But once four hundred guests arrived, the singers' voices disappeared about fifteen yards away.

Once you decide on your act, prepare contracts to sign. This will help you determine what equipment, power, and staging needs your performers require. Some will request special food and a place to go on breaks to rest. As with any other part of your event, give adequate recognition to the performers, including their names, photos, or other marketing material they provide. Their story can be part of your marketing for the event.

Accordion player Ry Burhans serenades guests as they join in singing.
Photo courtesy of Dan Kubus

Some fundraising events use famous performers as a draw. I've seen this done two ways. In a smaller community, think about whom you know who may be in touch with a well-known performer. Who in your community "made it"? They can present a case to the performer about your cause and ask them to support their "home town" by performing. With a name draw, you will be able to charge a much higher price. Or, you can hire the name act outright. This will be a large budget item, probably $5,000 to $50,000. Covering those high costs comes from sponsorship.

Find out how and when a performer must be paid and have that payment ready. Welcome entertainers at your event. Provide them with a hospitable place to get ready and relax during sets. And thank them for their great work. You might even be surprised by their generosity! They could become strong supporters of your cause.

Keep the entertainment fairly short or schedule it for the end of your event. A long, loud performance at dinner will drown out conversation. If it goes on too long, guests will start to leave. If you plan to speak or show a video at your event about your cause, stage the evening so that your message is placed prominently for best impact.

One of the better-received entertainers I've worked with traveled among the diners with his accordion taking requests. People loved it!

SUMMARY

1. Start early, especially if booking a name act. (One year out isn't too soon!)
2. Decide what type of entertainment will be appropriate to go with the theme of your event.
3. Ask someone in the know to recommend entertainers. If no one is available to help, go listen to some acts.
4. Approach the entertainer or their agent about availability and cost.
5. Negotiate what you will pay and what amenities you will provide, including meals, drinks, and special rest areas.
6. Communicate the entertainer's needs to the logistics committee.
7. Give an entertainer's publicity materials to the marketing committee.
8. Welcome entertainers to the event and make sure they have what they need.
9. Some acts may require payment ahead of time or at the event, so have those checks ready.

CHAPTER ELEVEN

Tell Your Story

COMMUNICATION

NOW THAT you have your event planned and ready to launch, how will you let your guests know who you are, what your cause is, and how they can help? Begin by considering how you will explain your cause and tell others about the upcoming event and the ways its profits will benefit that cause. Is there a tag line, an image, a description, or a catchy event name that will draw attention to you? People are bombarded with information about entertainment and opportunities to participate in their communities. Your job is to make people want to come to your event and support your cause.

So whom do you want to reach? Once you decide who your potential participants are, then you can decide how best to reach them. Are they public radio listeners? Parents? Sports fans? Each group will have specific ways they learn about events—in the newspaper, on the radio or television, through social media such as Facebook and Twitter, or on various websites. They may respond best to hearing about a fundraiser from a friend or colleague. Some folks learn about events through church, club, or team memberships. Be creative in using everything at your disposal to get the word out.

Your first contact with guests might be a "save the date" card or message. The purpose of this contact is to get your date on people's calendars so they reserve it for your event. Most communities have some type of calendar on which you can list an event. Most public media will list an event in the form of a press release or public service announcement. As there is no charge for this service, it usually is preferable to purchasing space or time, which can be quite costly. Include a very brief description of who you are and why you are hosting the event. Limit this message to two paragraphs, but include a story that tells about your cause. Be sure to state the basics of who, what, where, when, and why: who you are; what your cause is; what, when, and where the event will be held; why you are holding this event; who your partners are; and what your anticipated outcome will be. Conclude with a call to action and contact number.

Sending an invitation is another form of contacting prospective guests. You can mail a traditional printed invitation through the post or design an evite to be sent via email or another online messaging service. Include all the information guests will need to respond. Most online invitations allow for immediate registration and payment. If you're using a printed invitation, be sure to include a form, phone number, or email or website address— some way for people to sign up for your event. In your invitation, give your guests the opportunity to make an additional gift to your organization or cause.

As you work on your event, look for opportunities to share progress reports with your supporters and community. Are there photographic opportunities you could share or stories to tell? A big sponsor or celebrity guest could spur interest in your event. Ask your committee to post regular updates about the

One recipient speaks at the foodbank's annual meeting about the impact the donated funds had on her family. *Photo courtesy of Corey Longstreth*

fundraiser on social media sites. Call local broadcasters; ask if they will put your committee chair on-air to talk about the event to build support.

Your best chance to share your story in depth is at the event. Find a subtle way—one integrated into the fundraiser—to reinforce your message and call to action. At a race or golf tournament, set up a table with pledge cards or donation forms. Use lots of images to make the display large, dynamic, and exciting. Avoid a lot of text and academic or industry-laden language.

Hand out something guests can take home with them, consider, and act upon to show their support. Would shopping bags with your logo on them be appropriate? Are there other "branded" gift items you can share? Remember the weather, too. Wind or rain could demolish your display in a second!

An indoor event offers more ways to tell the story of your organization and cause. Again, displays are useful, but can be fairly flat and hard to see in a large crowd. A simple printed piece could be handed to guests, or placed at each individual's table seating. A rack card could be included in a small paper bag that also holds the place settings for dinner. A well-produced video is a great way to tell your story in an entertaining format, but keep it short—around three to five minutes. If it runs much longer, you'll lose your audience. We even texted the link to a video about our cause to guests during one event. We understood no one would watch it at the event, but we hoped they would look at it once they were home in a quiet location. Power point presentations have been used effectively to share images, but I recommend using them as background, not as speaking tools. No one enjoys reading a power point presentation—especially at a fundraising event.

You will need to thank your sponsors at the event. At the minimum, place their names and logos on a program, poster, or banner on display. If there is going to be a presentation, thank your guests and sponsors first, naming each individual sponsor correctly! Keep your speeches short; make sure you have a good spokesperson for your cause at the podium. Remember that the attention span of your guests is short. They will be wondering when dinner will arrive or when the dancing will begin.

Testimonials work well to tell a story about your cause. In place of the director, invite someone to speak who is a direct beneficiary of your cause, and ask that person to share what the work meant to him or her. Be sensitive to whom you are inviting concerning that individual's comfort level with speaking and being in an unfamiliar place. Don't exploit your beneficiaries; rather honor them and their contributions.

Posters are visually powerful, but they should be given secondary importance in your marketing strategy. There is less assurance that the targeted audience will really see them, let alone take action as a result. They can be used to reinforce a message, though, by providing a visual reminder of the date and location. However, huge, colorful banners are fairly affordable and can make a dramatic statement at your event. I have found these to be readily available from online sources.

Social media disperses information rapidly and cost effectively —an easy and great way for getting the word out about your event and reinforcing your message. Some programs, like Hoot Suite, will allow you to schedule messages and images through various platforms. Share details about the event planning and profiles of your leadership and emphasize the anticipated benefits and outcomes for your cause and community. Using as many platforms as you have access to will assure that all those who might consider participating in your fundraiser will get your message.

The best publicity will come from talking to the press and media about your event. Provide them with as much information as possible. Invite them to attend and report on the event. Provide photos that are of a quality high enough for publication. Unless your event is seeking to attract a large, general population, I don't recommend buying advertising to promote it. That is only worthwhile if you can find a sponsor to cover the cost of the ad. Some businesses have ongoing advertising contracts with local papers and will be happy to include your message in theirs.

Your best messaging, however, will come from your committee talking about their work with friends!

Finally, let everyone know what you've accomplished. Quantify your results if possible. Think about using infographics to illustrate the impact of your event on your community in terms of real change. Profile a recipient of the funds, such as a food pantry that, because of your fundraiser, can feed fifty more people a month. These facts will appeal to the heart of your donors and will prepare them to consider a possible future donation.

Evaluate the effectiveness of your message. Track how many people saw or heard your messages and where. A brief questionnaire sent to guests after the event asking for feedback could capture this information. Look at how many responded with a comment or donation. Adjust your plan based on these evaluations. This is a chance to show off the photos of those in attendance, the highlights of the event and even a "big check" hand-off to the recipient!

Include your story in your annual report!

SUMMARY

1. Plan your messages; include who you are, why you're doing this work, and who will benefit by the work.
2. Plan how you will tell your story: through social media, images, video, speakers, and testimonials.
3. Plan where to tell your story: print, social, or broadcast media; live; or on video.
4. Plan a schedule for release of your stories.
5. Implement this plan.
6. Evaluate your plan in terms of how many individuals were reached and the response and support it generated.

CHAPTER TWELVE

Make More Money

ADDING VALUE

LET'S LOOK at how you can increase income raised at your event. You've sold your tickets or collected your fees. You gave guests an opportunity to make additional donations on their registration forms. You have a robust list of sponsors who will cover the cost of your event and then some. You may even have a funding partner in the mix to boost income for your cause. What else can you do?

Auctions are a tried-and-true method to enhance revenue. An auction can be live with a real auctioneer, silent, or online. Live auctions will generate much more income than any other kind because guests enjoy watching and participating. They can see who is bidding against them and celebrate the winners—all feel a part of the event. Auctions can be wildly entertaining! When planning an auction, consider using a theme that would be appealing to your guests, something they would part with a lot of money to acquire. Successful items may include wine, travel destinations,

Professional auctioneers raise bids, keep items moving, and entertain.
Photo courtesy of Mathew Fratczak

original work by local artists, adventures such as horseback riding and parachuting, chef services for dinners in your home, parties (especially children's parties), and original, handmade jewelry. These items are all of high value or unique.

Use professional auctioneers. They know how to pitch an item, raise the bids, and process the bids once accepted. They are entertaining, as well. The songs they sing to sell an item comes from a unique skill honed with practice. They can even advise

The Rural Action Adventure Auction sells exciting experiences to eager bidders. *Photo courtesy of Kaitlin Owens*

you on what will sell, what won't, where to set your starting bids, and what valuable items should have a reserve price—a minimum bid needed to win. Our local auctioneer donates her services throughout the year to nonprofits in the region. She charms the money right out of guests' wallets. She makes bidding exciting, pitching bidders against each other with friendly banter, and often raising bids in the process.

To guarantee a successful auction, invite the right buyers, find donors for all your items, offer goods and services that people will pay high prices for, and contract the donated services of a professional auctioneer. Auctioneering is an art form! Some of the worst auctions I've attended were hosted by amateurs who showed little enthusiasm, had voices that didn't carry, and didn't know how to work the room, talk up a bid, build excitement and drama, and close a winning bid to benefit everyone. If you choose a live auction, go with the best! Avoid auction services—those companies who will "sell" you the items, then run your auction and take a big chunk (usually 50 percent) out of the proceeds.

Silent actions are held either in person at an event or online. An item is displayed and people write or submit their bids. They can see what the highest bid is and respond. Online auctions are becoming more popular. To hold one, you subscribe to a service for a small fee. The company will design your website, upload images and descriptions, process bids, and notify the winning bidders. Some fundraisers have successfully combined online with live auctions for a multidimensional event.

Raffles often complement live auctions. Tickets are sold for a chance to win an item—usually a bigger prize, such as a car or a pot of money—to attendees or to people in the community. One or several winners are drawn at the event or later. Split-the-pot events are a form of raffle where the ticket money goes into a pot and 50 percent is awarded back to the winners with the other 50 percent going to the cause. Be careful with raffles: in some states they are considered a form of gaming, and strict regulations exist concerning the sale or use of alcohol with gaming.

Auctions can ask for bids on cash donations; these are usually held last. For instance, a Planned Parenthood auction offered bidders the chance to sponsor five exams for $250, fifty pregnancy tests for $100, and other reduced-cost purchases of medical services.

Simply giving a donation form or envelope to each guest at the event can generate some additional funds and keep those guests connected to your organization and cause. Be sure to include the basics, such as the name of the check's recipient, your legal name, mailing and website address, and phone number, and request complete credit card information.

Golf tournaments can give their participants options to purchase mulligans (or one do-overs) per golfer. Merchandise such as T-shirts, mugs, cups, hats, bags, and posters can also generate extra income as long as the price is higher than the cost of the merchandise. Talent shows or similar events may allow people to use their checkbook to vote for the winners. There are many other

Silent auction items can bring additional revenue, but they should be carefully selected and presented well. *Photo courtesy of Brian Blauser*

ways to garner additional income at events. Use your creativity, know your community, and explore what else might work best for you and your cause.

SUMMARY

1. Do you need to raise additional income? If so, what approach would best fit your event and mission?

2. Any additional fundraising activity should offer a good profit margin to make it worth the time and effort involved.

3. Provide opportunities for your guests to make an additional contribution—at registration, during complementary activities such as auctions and raffles or voting at talent shows, and at checkout.

CHAPTER THIRTEEN

Now What?

SHARE YOUR RESULTS AND REMEMBER LESSONS LEARNED

THE EVENT is over, the results are in, but your work continues. No doubt you have learned many lessons along the way. If you've kept good records, it will be easy to adjust your course for the following year. Keep these records in an accessible notebook, on paper or stored digitally. Include everything you did, how you did it, and the lessons, thoughts, and ideas for improvement that you picked up along the way.

Over the years I've learned some lessons from my work. The first concerns food! Guests can be demanding. They can sometimes forget that the purpose of the event is to raise funds and behave as if they are at a five-star restaurant, demanding special treatment, seating, and food. They misbehave, drink too much, and take food and alcohol home with them. Your job is to *smile!* Always keep the big goal in mind: you are raising this money to help your community. If a guest's misbehavior is affecting others, try to speak to that guest quietly and calmly. It is your duty to cut off those who are drinking too much, and invite them to leave if they become disruptive.

Another challenge you may face concerns weather. Weather can laugh at the best of plans. It is impossible to ignore the part it plays in any outdoor event. Plan accordingly. Your choices include having a rain location that is inside, renting an enclosed tent, or having a rain date for rescheduling. If you let your guests know of last-minute weather changes in a timely manner you will allow for a smooth transition to plan B. We use our online program of events to notify guests of changes. Weather can impact indoor events as well. Know when you need to reschedule due to snow, ice, or flood. Don't put guests in jeopardy. I have never experienced a disaster due to weather, but I have had to cancel several annual meetings, and move an event inside when the weather was too hot and unpredictable.

Working with volunteers can be another delicate dance. Sometimes personal conflict rears its head in the group, or one individual seems determined to cause trouble. The best person to step in and have a conversation with the affected parties is the event chair. Loss of volunteers is not uncommon. You will more than likely have a committee member resign at some point, for any number of reasons. To avoid any disruption in your planning, assign several folks to each task. They can enjoy working together and, if one resigns, you are not left without someone heading an important function.

Become a seasoned conflict manager. At times conflict can arise when a committee member feels slighted. At other times a guest can feel ignored. Sometimes well-meaning volunteers spread misinformation behind everyone's back. The best way to work with these inevitable situations is to address them early and directly. As you work to build community, your transparency and willingness to work with everyone will be recognized; that will go a long way toward building goodwill. I now start my work with a group by going over the ways we will work together. We

At an event guests celebrate while building community.

Photo courtesy of Jo Carpenter

give everyone a voice at the table, we listen attentively and speak with intention, always mindful of our effect on the group. We support the work on the table and not necessarily individual agendas. With our work grounded in respect for all and a shared mission and vision, we have a sense of accomplishment and celebration in what we achieve together.

When members of the group respect one another, the more you plan for most scenarios, the smoother the ride will be when stuff happens. And stuff always happens! Ask wedding planners if they've ever had an event without a hiccup along the way! Make sure several people have a copy of the plans, including contacts' phone numbers and event logins. Keep your timelines, spreadsheets, and budgets up to date. Use a notebook to collect all of this, along with your observations, thoughts, and suggestions for the next chair or committee. Or use an online sharing mechanism such as Dropbox or Google docs. There is no need to reinvent the wheel each year if your event is repeatable.

And remember, this is sacred work. We are working together to build community by helping each other and celebrating who we are, where we come from, and what we care about in the process. Everyone will walk away with a new friend, a renewed spirit, and a sense of pride in the place they call home. Because we are fortunate to be able to help guide this work, it is important to thank people for what they offer and celebrate our success together. You'll probably agree that we have a lot to be thankful for.

Now it's time to tell your story. Begin by celebrating your success. Thank every person on the committee personally with a handwritten note, a celebratory party, or a phone call. Give modest thank-you gifts and lavish praise, and relive the event moment by moment. At your wrap-up party, take notes about what worked, what new ideas popped up, and what to scratch the next time. Use all this input when you start planning for the next year. Put these notes in your notebook.

FOODBANK DIRECTOR Katie summed up the impact this fundraiser has on our community. "Starting here a few years ago I was taken aback (to put it lightly) by how much work was suddenly in front of me. We not only had hurdles at our facility (in terms of staffing, efficiency, capacity, and overall financial stability) but to also come up with a plan to help all of our agencies with the same issues was pretty overwhelming. I knew what I needed to do with our facility and realized it would take time.

"I was unsure where to start with our agencies. Most of the operators were elderly, a lot of the facilities were in need of repair, and the lack of equipment they had was astonishing. They had not been given the tools needed to succeed and grow in quite some time, and any growth the foodbank had could not have been handled at their level. I was deeply concerned that we wouldn't be able to help enough of them in a short enough time to keep them (and us) sustainable.

"The first two grant cycles from Bounty on the Bricks completely addressed the most dire issues of our agencies in only two years. That still leaves me speechless. *Two years!* Plus, the process was simple for the agencies. Addressing the agency needs allowed me to turn my focus back to our needs, which is exactly where I need to be. The third cycle was icing on the cake. For the committee to first, ask; and second, understand and agree that what the agencies needed next was food was perfect."

Share your success with the community! Invite the media to your celebration. Write a press release touting your success and the impact this money will have on your cause. Make it personal; use testimonials. And thank yourself; give yourself a pat on the back. Celebrate your accomplishments so that you will feel renewed, recharged, and ready to do it again.

Immediately after your event, thank the donors! Every person at the event helped in his or her own way. Thank your guests with letters acknowledging their donations and telling them how they helped your cause. Thank your sponsors again and share the financial results and positive impact those funds had with them.

Although your event could be a wildly successful fundraiser, it may not last forever. The community may grow weary of the event. Sponsors may move on to other, newer, sexier events. Another trickier question the board may ask is how does this further our mission? Is the human capital spent on the event depleting other important work at the organization? These are hard decisions, but important ones, if you want your organization to remain viable and impactful. Continual evaluation will help you measure your successes and let you know if you reached your goal.

SUMMARY

1. Thank everyone who made the event a success.
2. Celebrate your success publicly.
3. Debrief on what worked and what didn't.
4. Share your notes, schedules, lists, and timetables in a notebook or shared online folder.
5. Evaluate the effectiveness of the event against your goals.
6. Decide whether to do it again.

CHAPTER FOURTEEN

Why We Do This

THE BIG PICTURE

FUNDRAISERS CAN become part of the fiber of your community. Through this work relationships and social capital are built on many levels: within the committee, with the wide variety of folks who attend, through the strong funders' collaborative that supports the work and the many sponsors who help out, to the beneficiaries that help or are helped to have better lives. Even the volunteers form a community for the duration of the project. Through this work, causes are affected positively, and those working toward those causes become a more connected and informed community.

One volunteer shared, "I feel like an important cog in the whole. Celebration is an important part of being human. It's key but it also takes our community forward by giving back. Fundraising events are a direct way to touch community and visibly inspire others to think bigger.

Fundraising strengthens community while helping others.
Photo courtesy of Jo Carpenter

"There is a good mix of people. We bring partners together for a common cause. Our collaboration generated different ideas than any one of us could have come up with on our own.

"It gives people power to put something like this together. I heard a few people say it's an event for the hoity-toity and not for common folks, that the event shuts people out. But I have seen the wide diversity at the table and I don't agree with this criticism."

In *Bowling Alone: The Collapse and Revival of American Community*, Robert Putnam describes the disconnectedness of our culture and the importance of building social capital or connections to stabilize communities. "Does social capital have salutary effects on individuals, communities, or even entire nations? Yes, an impressive and growing body of research suggests that civic

Cheryl Sylvester, Bounty on the Bricks event chair
Photo courtesy of Jo Carpenter

connections help make us healthy, wealthy, and wise."[1] "Social capital," he continues, "improves our lot . . . by widening our awareness of the many ways in which our fates are linked . . . Joiners become more tolerant, less cynical, and more empathetic to the misfortunes of others."[2] "To build bridging social capital requires that we transcend our social and political and professional identities to connect with people unlike ourselves."[3]

But why is community so important? How does building community make us stronger, feed more people, build connections, ease tension, and develop donors and volunteers? One of our committee members said, "It's an event that brings people together, reminds them of poverty, 'in the community.' We can solve problems quicker by working together."

Another shared, "We are a group that comes together, different groups at the same table, feeling proud about what we're accomplishing together. I so appreciate this community. This really

1. Putnam, *Bowling Alone*, 287.
2. Ibid., 288.
3. Ibid., 411.

BOUNTY CHAIR Cheryl has a talent for this work. She carefully nurtures and respects the autonomy of every committee member. They, in turn, love her. In fact, three years ago she won the local Red Cross Hometown Hero Award for her work on Bounty. But she would say, as much as she gives, she receives back more.

After the start of the second year, Cheryl was diagnosed with breast cancer. She had worked hard over the last three years to gain back her strength and mobility from a crippling attack of Guillian-Barre Syndrome, a disease that attacks the peripheral nervous system causing rapid weakness in the limbs. The first year chairing Bounty she had gained back enough strength and muscle control to resume driving. Yet the disease lingered in her gait, her energy level, and her muscle strength.

When we received the news of her cancer diagnosis, we were devastated. How could such a joyful person be plagued with so much ill health? Yet she soldiered on. She continued to lead her team while enduring chemo treatments. She sported multicolored headscarves and kept us all going. We had become a community. Our work together went beyond simply hosting a party or raising money: it built strong social capital to support the individual, the team, and our community. Cheryl said of that time, "Personally, it took my mind off my treatments for breast cancer."

represents the best of us, what is unique about us . . . a close-knit community coming together for a good meal and a good cause."

Putnam states, "Size of community makes a difference: formal volunteering, working on community projects, informal helping behaviors (like coming to the aid of a stranger), charitable giving, and perhaps blood donations are all more common in small towns than big cities. Social recluses are rarely major donors or active volunteers, but schmoozers and machers are typically both."[4]

4. Ibid., 119.

Fundraising events build social capital in a community. Through a year of planning, committee members make new friends. They support each other through struggle. They learn new skills and laugh together. They focus for a while on providing a great experience for guests and on raising funds to help their community.

The benefit to the organization goes beyond the visibility in the community. The web of connections is strengthened for friends, volunteers, donors, guests, and sponsors. Your credibility has increased. You said what you would do, you did it, and it worked! That can serve as a vehicle to grow the organization. New donors are accessed who can be invited to participate in other ways with the work of the organization. Your goal is to move these guests along a fundraising continuum to eventually become donors to the organization.

Has Bounty on the Bricks strengthened our community? I think so. More money sits in the bank accounts of food pantries throughout the region. Committee members gained new skills and made new friends and connections in the community. We may have even raised the threshold of excellence and levels of partnerships for other local organizations wanting to try new avenues of fundraising.

I hope this book has given you some good ideas to support your fundraising goals. Events can be great fun! Good luck!